THE DAYDREAMING MOGUL'S GUIDE VOLUMES 1 & 2

Niem Green

The Day Dreaming Mogul's
Guide
Volumes 1 & 2:
Daydreams and Success / Credit Score Dating - The Sexiness of
Credit
By Niem Green

A Green Walk Media Publication
A Green Walk Industries Company
Wilmington, DE
Copyright © 2009, ©2016, and ©2017
by Niem M. Green

Green Walk Media
A Green Walk Industries Company
Dover, Delaware, USA

The Daydreaming Mogul's Guide Volumes 1 & 2: Daydreams and Success / Credit Score Dating - The Sexiness of Credit by Niem M. Green

To the beautiful and influential women in my life, past, present and future.

Contents

A WORD FROM THE AUTHOR

Daydreams, Love, and Success all comes down to vision.

The vision of your dream so pure that you act it out by day. The vision you share with a love so explicitly that nothing can separate you. That love that may be the only person that doesn't think you're crazy or they could be crazy right along with you because they can see your vision. Even more impressive they share the same vision. No negative force can hinder you. No argument, no hardship, and no temptation can stop you 2 because the vision is clear and the focus is the vision.

The success of achieving that vision. Especially, realizing that vision with your love. The success of feeling the moment of sanity and peace in a chaotic world. The success of returning the investment of time, support, and energy in your love that supported you. The success of saying "we weren't that crazy after all.

This is Vision and Vision is Daydreams, Love, and Success. This is why I am The The Day Dreaming Mogul. I help others to find their vision. Whether creditscoredating, Style My Date, Daydream Financial, or Interactive Daydreams. From love to money, books to dating sites and everything in between I help people find their vision.

A man with daydreams needs a woman with a vision

Niem M. Green - The Daydreaming Mogul

PART I - DAYDREAMS AND SUCCESS

INTRODUCTION

In life, there are a few words that no matter how we apply them or who we are they are contained in all of our vocabularies. These words are success, dreams, and goals. We may have a dream of living a carefree life, gauge our success by our material possessions. We may have goals to spend more time with our families; these three words tend to run our lives.

It doesn't matter if you are an executive at a Fortune 500 company, self-employed McDonald's franchise owner, a janitor at the local bank, or a housewife, you have dreams, goals, and an opinion of what success means to you. This book is a guide to show you how to put these things together to help you to accomplish virtually anything you want.

Before we get started, I want to make a few disclosures. 1. This is not a gimmick; I will not make promises of fame and fortune. As with anything that is worth having, it is going to take work. 2. I am not a psychologist or psychiatrist, nor will I claim to be. 3. Everything I share in this book I have put in to practice and observed in people who are successful by their definitions of success. This guide illustrates merely a way to think to help you to achieve the things that you want the most.

In most of our lives, we're told many things; however, two of this statements tend to stick with us. They are: You can do whatever you put your mind to, and if you believe in yourself, you can be whatever you want to be. These are two powerful and positive statements, and to a certain degree, they are correct. The thing about them is while we are told these words, we are not told how actually to execute them and use them in our lives. Some of us have subconsciously, but most of us have not. Going back to the three words we discussed earlier, dreams, goals, and success, these three words are important in utilizing these statements. However, what do they mean? Their definitions will be critical in applying these statement to our everyday lives.

Let us first look at the word "Dream". When we hear this word, we automatically associate it with something that is not real. We use it to give us purpose in life and the things that we do from day to day. For example, "I'm going to school to get my "dream" job as a lawyer. On the other hand, I am moving toLA to better my chances of making my "dream" come true of being a blockbuster actor or actress. The dictionary defines the word dream as a series of thoughts, images, and sensations occurring in a person's mind during sleep. This definition implies that dreams occur only during sleep. We will leave this for now, but we will revisit this and expand upon it later in this book.

The next word we are going to look at is "Goal." Many times, we use the word goal synonymously with the word dream; yet, the dictionary defines a goal as the object of a person's ambition or effort; an aim or desired result. The word goal is completely different from the definition of a dream. The definition of dream implies lack of action while the definition of goal implies alertness. This is because these definitions are biased to the user perception of the words. Do not worry, by the time you finish this book you will have a new perception and possibly a new definition of the words.

Finally, "Success," this word is probably the most inconsistent when it comes to its definition. The dictionary defines success as"the accomplishment of an aim or a purpose". If I ask you what success means some of you will say "having a good job," while others will say, "being financially free," and then there are some who will say "Having an empty nest, raising our children and ensuring they have a good start in the world." While all of these definitions vary, they are not wrong, they still have the basic definition from the dictionary, yet they are expanded and personalized to fit one's life. For me, success is different for all types of people the result differs based on the ingredients and tools used.

This is very similar to baking a cake. If you take three different people, give them access to the same pantry, and tell them to bake a cake to the best of their ability with no instructions, you will get three very different cakes. Nonetheless, you will get three cakes.

From an early age, we are taught, and we learn different ways to become successful. Let me correct that, we are taught different definitions of success and advised of the different tools to obtain success. One of the most common examples of this are to be successful you have to go to college and get a good job. Some argue that some of the most successful people in the world did not finish college or even high school. Regardless of which path they took; they are successful by either their standards or someone else's.

The common factor is that they had dreams and goals, which resulted in their success.In my life, travels, and dealing with the public, I have had the privilege of getting to know people from all walks of the earth and life. From the fortunate to the unfortunate, the poor to the rich, and the formally educated to the informally educated, while these are very different people in their right, they are still very similar in that they all again contain the same three words in their vocabularies.

These observations have helped me to identify a particular formula or tool to accomplish whatever it is you want to accomplish. This tool, yet very powerful it'snot the end all be all, and it is simple, in fact, it is so simple we do it subconsciously, and don't know that we do it.

It is "Daydreaming," at this point; you are more than likely looking at this page funny and wondering what in the world, I am talking about, and what does daydreaming have to do with dreams, goals, and success. You are more than likely thinking like this because of the common perception that daydreaming is wasting time and nonproductive.

In fact, the dictionary defines daydreaming as "a series of pleasant thoughts that distracts one's attention from the present.I will prove to you that daydreaming, when used correctly will not enhance the likelihood of reaching your goal but also enhance your definition of success. When I daydream my goals are defined, and the tools required to achieve said goals become identified. After reading this book,you will be able to do the same.

CHAPTER ONE - IT'S ALL IN YOUR MIND

To fully take advantage of and understand "Daydreaming," you must first understand the key components. In the next few chapters, we will review all of these components. The first that we will review is the place where all the magic happens, the mind. The mind is truly incredible, and it is something that we all have. It is important that we do not make the common misperception that the mind and the brain are one in the same.

The brain powers the mind just like every other part of the human anatomy. The mind is conceptual rather than physical. The dictionary defines mind as "the element of a person that enables them to be aware of the world and their experiences." While it defines the brains "an organ of soft nervous tissue in the skull of vertebrates, functioning as the coordinating center of sensation and intellectual and nervous activity." Therefore, the mind conceptually lives in the brain. In looking at the definition of the mind, it is almost unbelievable to realize that each one of us encompasses such a power.

Anupa Kumar Patri in his book M-Power, published September 29, 2011, states that "the mind refers to aspects of intellect and consciousness manifested as combinations of thought, perception, memory, emotion, will, and emotions including all the brain's conscious and unconscious cognitive processes." This means that the mind has the ability to control a person's body, feelings, and actions.

While to a certain degree we are able to control our minds, there is still a part of our mind that we have not used. That is truly making our minds work for us. A way to understand the mind is by thinking of it as a computer. Computers run simply by input and output, that is, you input information or a query and your computer calculates and processes the input and outputs as the response, answer, or action. The difference between that and our mind is that our minds never cut off. The mind is constantly receiving input and outputting info to cause actions, feeling, emotions, etc. With the right control of your mind, you can do whatever you put it too.

Hence, the saying "you can do anything you put your mind to." Much like a computer, it is not as simple as turning it on and telling it to do something. In the case of the mind, you cannot just think something especially something big and expects it to happen.

This is where many of us are misled. For example, you may have the most powerful on the market to date, but with an out an operating system like Windows or Macintosh OSX, you would have no idea how to use its power. Therefore, our computers come with software to control the hardware. Even with the software for your computer to do what, you want you to have to use the correct commands with the correct software.

Turn on your computer and when it loads type on the computer play a game. What happens? Well unless you have your computer programmed to recognize such a command without using a program, nothing happens. The same is true with our minds, think to yourself to do something like write a hit song or make a million dollars. What happens? Well if you are not a hit songwriter or a person who makes money at will your not going to do it. Do not get me wrong; I am not saying it is not possible, what I am saying is, however, our minds need to be properly programmed to do the things we want especially on a large scale.

By the end of this book, you will have the ability to program your mind to do several things, all of which will assistyou to reach or enhance your idea of success.

Do you remember the saying a mind is a terrible thing to waste? That statement is very true especially when you think of all that your mind controls, and its abilities. Just as your mind can do so many positive things, it can also do very negative things to harm yourself or someone else. While we know that this is true consciously, it is alsotrue subconsciously. Remember, your mind is your mind; it will do anything you tell it to do good or bad. Not too many people realizethat.

The saying "death is in the tongue" is not ultimately correct; "death is in the tongue that controls the mind." If you keep, negative thoughts whether it is for a show, for attention genuinely because you are in a negative place in your life, you will program your mind to be negative. A person who thinks of death and negativity will more than likely have negative experiences with high chances of having a premature end. For this reason, it is best policy and practice to think positive thoughts and indeed make the best of a negative situation. I know this sounds cliché, but taking into account the power of the mind it is a warning that should be heeded.

There is another cautious word about the health and well being of the mind. By now, you may have noticed my references and comparison to computers when it comes to the mind. This is for two reasons; the computer actually uses the same concept and processes as the mind, and the computer was based on it. Also, almost everyone has a computer, so it is easy to explain with a relevant medium that all of us are familiar. What happens when your computer is not maintained correctly? It slows down and itloses its relevance. The same is accurate with the mind. One of the main concerns that consumers have with computers is that after a short period it becomes obsolete. While we cannot replace our minds, ways of our thinking change over the course of time, different processes evolve allowing for stimulating ideas to come to the forefront.

Look at the technological timelines with phones and computers. Here's a quick example of both: First it was the computer, then the user-friendly OS or "Windows," then the world wide web, then e-mail, etc. The phone was invented, then, the facsimile, then mobile phones, then text messaging, etc. Now with both of these time lines therewere many additions and variances like yourMyspace, Google, Facebook, VOIP, etc. Nevertheless, it was a few ideas that kept feeding the public minds, when other mind collected the input they were calculated, and the output results were different variances, inventions, ideas, and concepts. A lot of money was made and is still being made, and it all branched off a few different minds.

The key is to ensure that your mind is fresh with current input. For instance, magazines are not solely for entertainment and ad revenue. A magazine is filled with an array ofstimulating colors, picture, and ideas. While you may be reading a magazine to learn about what is going on in Hollywood or Sim Valley, your mind will subconsciously absorb input that has nothing to do with either topic but can be very useful and stores it for later use.

The problem is people do not think of it or useit and it winds up in a mental recycle bin. We will speak of this later, and you will know how to control what your mind inputs and what to do with it.

In review, the mind is a super computerthat has no instructions. We learn how to use it as we grow and the software or programming that we develop comes from the surroundings that we are raised. Some common softwareor programming examples are our manners, the schooling and career paths that we choose, and the way we live our lives as good and badcitizens. Those of us with children take theresponsibility of programming our children'sminds. We ought to be mindful of this, as the children indeed are our futures.

CHAPTER TWO - GARBAGE IN, GARBAGE OUT, FILTERING YOUR INPUT

Now that you have some idea of the power of the mind, it is essential to understand the importance of screening what things the mind inputs. I can remember when I was younger; my mother said something to me that would stick with me forever. That is "Garbage in garbage out." She told me no matter what I do in life I get what I put into it.

For instance, with a bank account, if I put little money in the account, I could take small money out whereas if I were to put no money into it, I could not take money out. If I did garbage work for school, I should expect garbage grades.

The same concept applies with the mind. Remember that the basis of the mind's operation is input and output. The world is full of data and as it is not a perfect world all the information available is not ideal. Thinking of the mind again as a computer, some of the most essential software that your computer contains are antivirus, spam guards, and firewalls. These things protect your computer from harmful and sometimes fatal viruses, programs, etc.

The same applies to our minds; we must protect it from such things as well. These things are not in the form of computer viruses and spam but in the way of harmful input. Such input can be dangerous and fatal to our minds. Now things are not always deadly to the mind, but one of the most hurtful things that can affect our minds are distractions and negativity.

Think of distractions as pop-ups on the Internet. How many times have you been online and you are looking specifically for something or at a website, and you are bombarded by tons of pop-ups. These pop-ups could mean well in some instances, but they slow down your productivity and distract your focus.

The same applies to life; many of us are sidetracked from accomplishing goals by distractions. These distractions can come in the form of people, seemingly great opportunities, or even or wants. I am not saying lock yourself in a cave and become a hermit. I am stating you have to explicitly identify these things and moderate them accordingly. Maintain your focus on your task. Develop a mental pop-up blocker and firewall to help reduce and govern your minds exposure to such things.

The most significant filter that your mind needs is similar to an anti-virus program as previously mentioned. My mother used to tell me so many things as a child, one of the things that she was persistent in instilling in me was the biblical verse, "Bad association spoils useful habits." I have watched so many people fall victim to this saying. Some of my best friends who could have and would have been great athletes, scientists, businessmen, and entertainers have fallen to the perils of lousy association and input.

Remember, our minds are continually receiving input. We can never shut it off at best we can filter and monitor it. Remember your mind calculates your wants,needs, and desires and subconsciously putstogether a way to satisfy these things.

Here is a story that should put this into better perspective for you. A young boy lived in an impoverished neighborhood. His family was destitute, at night he could not sleep due to the fighting and crying about money that he heard his parents going through. He paid it no attention until one day he asked his mom for a new video game system. His mother broke down in front of him, which was unusual because in front of her children his mother had a steady demeanor holding all her pains and anxieties in and would let them out at night while they slept.

Well, this day was different, she broke down crying and told him that she barely had money to feed the family. This registered with the boy and suddenly all the fighting and screaming at night came to his mind he realized this is what causes his lack of sleep. His parents were out of money, and this is what caused his parents pain. His eyes began to tear up a little and went outside to play with his friend.

His friend and his family seemed to do well. The young boy never cared or wondered why his friend had money and all of the things until this day. He found himself asking many questions until eventually, it clicked. The result was that the boy started selling drugs with his friend for his friend's family.

This may seem like a stretch, but it is often the ugly reality of our inner city youth. The boy's mind put several things together, why his parents were in pain, the problem and solution.

Unfortunately, the boy had no filters, his mind did precisely what it was supposed to do. His mind received the input, "lack of money causes his family pain," made him alert to things in his surroundings that did not stand out to him before. His friend had everything he wanted, and his family was happy", the reasoning of the differences, "The friend and his family sold drugs," and produced the solution or output, "I can sell drugs too."

This could have turned out many different ways. Remember in the introduction the example of the cake. The cake that was made in this instance was an ugly one. However, let's change up some of the ingredients.

Understand again that this is nota perfect world so there will be a lot of negative input that we receive. For the sake of this example what we will change in the story, is the friend. Let's say the friend's family was still well to do. However, this was because the friend did some odd jobs around the neighborhood for extra money, like a paper route, cutting grass, and helping his father down at his shop. Theoutput that the boy would have had would bemuch more positive.

This example demonstrates two principal types of input, the association that we keep and the ideas and surrounding that we are exposed to. Let's assume that the boy did not have a friend so to speak or he did, but somewhere in his surroundings, he got the idea to just take the things he needed from others such as his friend. We would then have the birth of a thief on the early criminal track.

Let us look at another saying, "Misery love company." Many of us use this saying but do we know what it means or entails. This much like the saying mentioned previously "bad association spoils useful habit," Can be used as a filter.

From my mother, I knew that if I hung around with people that did immoral things I would, in turn, do unethical things. Such is true with, "misery loves company," If we know that, then we know to expect miserable input from miserable people.

Too many times I hear people say this, but they continue hanging around miserable people. This would be OK if the goal were to help the discontented become more positive or the unhappy person was receptive to positivity. A person that hangs around a miserable person will eventually become miserable if the mental filters are not adequately set and the mind is not properly conditioned.

I cannot stress this enough, your subconscious will receive the negative input from the miserable person. It will then calculate the similarities in your life, and the output will result in becoming miserable. No matter how happy you have been with your life before your encounter with the unhappy person, you will find something wrong with it and begin to look at it through a negative light.

This is similar to the saying "The glass is half full or half empty." It is all in your perception, and negative people can cause an adverse impression while the reverse is true.

Granted, we deal with miserable people every day, not all of us become miserable subconsciously we have filters in place, and our positivity will be stronger than the misery, which is good.

My goal is that you are now aware of this guard and use it productively as filtering your input is a crucial component to daydreaming.

In review, the data is everywhere, and it can be in the form of people, ideas, activities, etc. We must filter the things that we input to ensurethat we have positive outputs. We should make sure that we have mental pop-up blockers, firewalls, and anti-viruses in place to protect our minds.

CHAPTER THREE - ROOM TO THINK

One of the most essential components in daydreaming is a space to think or daydream. Now this area should be in a positive environment that is not biased to any particular thought unless it has something to do with what you are thinking. This space should be relaxing butnot promoting of sleep.

The key is to dream with open eyes and actually going to sleep and dreaming defeats your purpose. Remember this is time for you and your mind, so you do not want to have people with you, not a child, friend, lover, husband, wife, etc. This is your time to calibrate your mind and set your focus. Eventually when you find your perfect place to set your ideal balance, you will be able to revisit it virtually in your mind at will.

This comes in handy if you are a busy person like me. I have trained my mind to escape to my "happy place" at will. When I am under a lot of pressure, have a deadline to meet, need to come up with a good idea, or just need to get away in the middle of the day without physically getting away, I use a trigger to visit this place in my mind.

Let's discuss these triggers; these triggers can be anything that you can program your mind to identify. I like to think of these triggers as the doorbell to the dream room.

For me personally, it is music. There are a few songs that no matter, where I am or what I am doing if I play them, I will go into a daydream. I do not want you to get the wrong idea, a daydream it not some type of high, trance, or even sleep. It is merely a mental alertness. This allows you to focus on whatever you need or want. We will visit the daydream very soon.

Triggers are things that stimulate yourmind to think about the things you need orwant to think. These triggers should do two things; the first is to boost your mood. You need to be able to create enthusiastically also, positively.

Think of when you workout if you work out. You generally play an uptempo song to amp you. That is to stimulate you to promote your energy level. On the other hand, think of another setting, think of setting the mood for a date. Generally, you would put on a song that is slow and subtle like "Moments in Love" by The Art of Noise. Like the perfect score in a movie to a love scene, this song stimulates the mood.

The music guides the flow of your date or in some cases your lovemaking. Similarly, a conventional trigger would be a song that would stimulate the mood you are aiming for.

The other trigger is generally something visual. Whether you are currently doing the work or something, you are planning. You want things around you that stimulate your mind in the direction you are aiming. This could be your result or something that reminds you of the goal you are attempting to accomplish.

I have seen people use pictures of their families, pictures of something they are hoping to attain, and pictures of things they wish to buy. There is no rule to what this canor cannot be. It all depends on what stimulates you and your mind.

This will be the first time that most of you will consciously daydream. I recommend finding a quiet place whether it is your car, the park, your deck, bathroom, bedroom, wherever, take only a pen and paper. Find some music that relaxes you again not putting you to sleep but merely calms you.

Sit and listen to your music and try not to think. You will not literally stop thinking, but you will hear your mind. Focus in on your thought and what it is presenting to you. Now write down the thingsthat you can see or hear mentally.

Remember from chapter one the mind is able to utilize all of your senses virtually. Therefore, it is possible that you will be able to smell things and taste things as well as hearing, seeing and feeling.

Write these things down, the things that you present themselves the most, naturally are what is on your mind. After you finish writing and if it has not bestowed itself ask yourself, "what do I want the most?" Your subconscious will tell you or show you, again write it down. If you are able to do this, you have found your balance and your place.

Keep a visual picture of this place, as you will be able to return to it in your mind. Remember the total environment, the temperature, the song playing, etc. If you have not found the place try again, try a different song, or another area. The setting that you initially found may not be right for this exercise. Most of us already have aplace though it is not thought of as a place todaydream but as a place to relax or get away.

Some of you may feel that no such place exists; I assure you it does, even if just for this instance. Remember ultimately you are findinga piece of mind. This peace of mind is valuable in not just daydreaming but in functioning. Many of us get overwhelmed because we do not find peace of mind. I assure you once you literally discover this peace of mind that you can escape. You will notice a change in your demeanor and overall quality of life.

It will be harder to become stressed out.

CHAPTER FOUR - I MUST BE DREAMING

Finally, we get to one of the most essential components to daydreaming, which is the dream. Remember from the introduction that dreaming is defined as "a series of thoughts, images, and sensations occurring in a person's mind during sleep." in the dictionary. We are going to remove the "during sleep" from the definition and focus on the actual dream. Dreaming is your mind processing and analyzing your thoughts. In other words, it is actually thinking very intensely.

Think of a time when you had a dream that felt so real that you woke up looking for people or things that were in your dream. Generally, things that affect you the most trigger dreams like this. Such as wants, desires, needs, pain, joy, etc. To manage your dream is to truly harness and control the power of your mind.

As I indicated previously when I dream, I see my result of what I want to do or where I want to be. This is not limited merely to my creative efforts and ventures, such as my novels and film projects. This is also true for the logistics of all of my businesses.

Before I start a company or enter a business venture. I dream of every aspect of the situation from a-z. Actually, it's more like from z to a. Let me explain, my dreams start with the end result, and it is then broken down step by step as to how I got there or what actions and things in place caused the effect. I apply this to the consciousworld follow the steps. Moreover, would reach the desired outcome.

Now I must say that while we strive for some things or results, it is not guaranteed that things will end up precisely how we planned. This is OK because you will be close enough where you can push a little harder or tweak a little, and you're there. For some people being that close means you came, a long way and that desired satisfaction are enough.

I was told when I was younger, "always aim for 100 because 90 isn't bad" I honestly believe this. Think of the 90 out of 100 in terms of money. Let's say you strive to earn $100 million and you make $90 million. How will you feel? You should still feel a sense of pride and success in that you are within an arm's length of your actual goal. This means that when you try again if you do not choose to settle, you will only need to aim for 10, or if you strive for 100 again and get 90, you will be at $180 million overshooting your goal by $80 million.

Now stop grinning let us get back to the dream. For your dream to ultimately guide you to things that you want, you must know what you want. Many of us are aimlessly roaming day to day, just getting by and doing things out of habit rather than for purpose. This it nothing to be ashamed of it is OK.

You have to take the time a figure out what exactly you want to do with yourself or for yourself. Take some time as in the last exercise and figure it out. More than likely, it is there, you just have not paid enough attention to hear or see what it is. Your mind knows however. All you have to do is focus in on it.

Some people will argue that dreams are out of our control. I beg to differ; most people have not made a conscious effort to dream.

Consider this, what happens when we watch a scary movie? We tend to have nightmares or a dream that has some sort of reflection of what we saw in the film. This is more common in children as their minds are not as full as adults with things to do or responsibilities.

Going back to the first chapter, remember that the mind takes in the input, calculates and processes it and produces output. Well as children we don't have prioritized output. Hence, we don't have to worry about paying bills or going to work or raising other children, so their minds take the most exciting or stimulating thoughts such as the scary movie and focus mainly on that. This then produces the nightmare.

Now as an adult if the main thought priority is our goal and we condition our minds accordingly by stimulating these thoughts, we will dream of whatever it is. To accustom our thoughts in preparation for the proper dream, we must influence our mind, which is giving it input to process and calculate.

For example, when I was younger, my dream job was to become an investment banker. I can remember watching movies like "Wall Street" before going to bed. I would then dream of being a high power broker on Wall Street.

When you do something or watch something that you already have an interest in, your mind processes that information comparatively to your personal situation to allow you to visualize yourself in that scenario. Paying close attention to this enables you to identify the key things in those surroundings that let you see what is needed to make that dream or vision a reality.

Of course, there are limits, I am not saying if you watch Superman and dream of being Superman, paying attention to how his suit is made will allow you to create one and you will be able to fly. However, you may come up witha great story or film idea of your own.

Dreams are great because they make your thoughts visual and vivid. It is like creating a movie with an endless budget. Anything you can see, feel touch, taste, or hear while your awake, you are able to in your dream. Your mind uses all of the things that you encounter or thinks of during the day to play a movie while you sleep. This is something that we can take advantage of whenever we like.

I can remember having such vivid dreams as a child that I would want to sleep. I got to a point where I could literally dream of whatever I wanted. Even things and places that I never experienced I could dream about in detail. I did not know at the time, but I controlled my mind and dream by exploring books, pictures, TV, and movies.

I can still do this now, but I much rather dream during the day vividly about things I am attempting to accomplish. After all, I am the "Day Dreaming Mogul."

CHAPTER FIVE - GET FOCUSED, START DAYDREAMING

B efore we get started on one of the most important chapters in this book, let us quickly review what we learned thus far. Our minds are our computers that receive input, calculate it, and produce output.

Input can be defined as anything in a person's surroundings including people, places, things, events, etc. Output can be described as an action, thought, feeling, emotion, etc. triggered by your mind. The types of input, whether negative or positive will produce output that will be parallel to the input, negative or positive. We must use this information to filter the input we are exposed.

We should find a neutral place that allows us to relax and listen or watch what our minds are telling us. Once we determine this area and we are able to clearly identify what our thoughts are telling us, we should detail the things that inspired that moment of clarity. Upon identifying these triggers, we should then be able to trigger these things in our minds at any given time or place, which will allow us to return to the place of clarity in our minds.

Finally, dreams are products of our minds thinking intensely.

We can condition our minds to fashion our dreams to guide us to the things we want the most. Before we dream we should ensure that, we are surrounded by input that stimulates our minds in the direction of what we want or need to dream of. Therefore, with this, you should have a good understanding of your mind's ability and dreams.

Now it is time bring it together and discuss "Daydreaming". Remember the dictionary definition of the daydream is "a series of often distracting and usually pleasant thoughts and images that pass through the mind while awake."

The dictionary gives daydreaming the connotation of being nonproductive or distracting. As I indicated, we are now going to redefine the term "Daydream." So, from this point on forget the old definition of the word.

When we dream again, our great minds are busy at work calculating and processing input that we received to produce images, senses, thoughts, feelings, emotions, etc. Imagine if you could harness the power of your mind that is powerful enough to rouse your body's actions and your thoughts during your sleep, while you are conscious. Well you can, this is daydreaming.

To understand daydreaming let's look at the quote from T.E. Lawrence. "Those who dream by night in the dusty recesses of their mind wake to find that it was all vanity, but those who dream by day are dangerous men for they may act out their dream with open eyes."

This quote is one that I live by because it has a genuine significance in my life. This is because it totally makes sense. When I firstheard this quote, I was intrigued. I never thought of the power of a dream and actually doing it while being awake.

Most people have astounding dreams that are meaningful, descriptive, and tell us things. The problem is most of us forget them by thetime we realize that we even have them. Even the best dreams that we have that are vivid and are so real that we awaken looking for things in our dreams, we tend to forget details.

Sad to say this is why most of us do not achieve or live out our dreams. This is not because we are not capable because we are. We do not reach our dreams, contrarily because we do not remember them or specific details that are needed to achieve them. Sounds like a simple reason not to fulfill a dream, right? Well, simple problems are solved by simple solutions.

The solution is to dream during the day, that is, envisage while we are conscious.

Now let me be very clear in my explaining of this. You will be entirely conscious while you daydream. You will not be in a trance or anything of the sort. This method of daydreaming solely allows your conscious and subconscious mind interact to aid you in whatever task you wish to achieve.

Some of you will get the connotation that daydreaming only implies to achieving goals that have to do with owning businesses and gaining fame etc. However, a daydream can be large or small, it could have to do with anything remember it is all about you, the things you want, and the things that matter to you the most. Daydreaming is utterly a tool to help you get from point A to point Z by way of points B, C, D, etc.

At very least your daydream should be a roadmap that shows you the points and how to connect them. Now, the points depend on what you determine them to be. For example, a salesperson would daydream about reaching or exceeding a particular sales goal. An executive may daydream about how to make his or her business unit more effective and efficient. While a business owner may daydream about expanding or downsizing to reach a profitability goal.

Regardless who you are or what you do, the possibilities are limitless when you daydream. Single parents can daydream of ways to balance work and home, while homemakers can daydream of a smoothly ran household. Daydreaming is an equal opportunity tool. The beauty of it is yours, and it is custom tailored to fit your life and your aspirations.

CHAPTER SIX - WHAT COMES FIRST, THE DAYDREAM OR THE GOAL

Now that you know how to control your dreams and mind as well as what it means to daydream. Most of you are anxious to get started, which is excellent, while some will pose the question "how to get started?" The truth is you already have, subconsciously.

The task is to consciously do it adequately to achieve your goals. Goals, this should pose the question" what to do first, set the goal or daydream?" Well again, this depends on you. Asks yourself, "What are my goals?" If you do not know, then you have some daydreaming to do. Think back to chapter 3, take some time to yourself, and figure out what it is that you want or need.

Just a sidebar, I actually call this processing "green storming," but that is just me. Once you know what it is you want, whether it is love, family, money, career, material things, etc. Write it down; with this, you can join us for the next step. This step is conditioning, remember to dream or efficiently daydream you must control the input that your mind receives.

Now that you know what your focus is, find all the things that have to do with it. Whether it is pictures, songs, movies, TV shows, websites, etc. List these things, and one by one implement them in your life. For example, the pictures should now become screen savers on your computers and phones or placed in areas that you spend most of your time. Your iPods or music devices should contain the songs that are relative or inspire you to think of what you want.

The movie is now in your collection and if or when you have a chance to watch TV you're watching it as opposed to Desperate Housewives or Sports Center unless these shows have to do with your goal or inspire that thought process. While I'm not saying create your goals a shrine in every facet of your life, I am, however, saying to fit your target into your life so that subconsciously while you're in your conscious world. The daydream can be incited at every avenue of your life, no matter what you are doing or where you are.

Eventually, you will not need as much stimulation to daydream. These triggers will be in your mind, and the stimulus will be automatic. The time to clearly daydream and see yourself reaching your goals varies on you and a few other variables. So if you do not begin vividly daydreaming immediately, it is OK. Remember your mind is used to having two separate thought processes that are, conscious and subconscious in two separate worlds.

What you are doing is again using the analogy of the computer is, upgrading your operating system. For those of you who have done this know that this can take a while depending on how old your computer is and how many things and programs are currently on your computer. With this in mind be patient it will occur.

While I understand entirely that most of us have busy lives that do not readily allow us to take days off and clear schedules. I recommend if possible taking a day and clearing your agenda. Use your phone only for emergencies and focus on you. This will expedite the process of upgrading your mind to a daydreaming operating system.

On this day, you will need your list of goals, triggers, and the things that inspire relaxation in your life. Focus on each item one by one and look at or listen to the corresponding trigger that represents accomplishment of this goal to you. Take your time with each; you are painting a mental picture in your head of achieving your goals. In this image, you want to identify every detail of that moment when you accomplish each goal. The power of your mind will eventually help finish the mental picture for you. Once the picture is complete, you will see yourself is that surrounding. Your job then will be to pay close attention to what is in those surroundings that help you achieve each goal.

CHAPTER SEVEN - REACHING YOUR DREAM TAKES LUCK

By now you should feel confident that you will reach goals and become successful, that is by your definition of success. Do not fret your idea of success will be defined in your daydream if it is not already defined for you.

While I may be a great motivator, speaker, and writer, it is impossible for me to define success for you. As again, you and your goals determine your success. While daydreaming is powerful, it is just one tool that you need to reach your goals.

You will also need luck, not luck defined by the dictionary as, "Success or failure brought on by chance, rather than one's own actions." However, luck defined by the quote by Roman philosopher, Seneca, "Luck is when preparation meets opportunity." In other words, no matter what your goals are or how you define success, you must always be prepared.

Many people look at those who are successful and say that they are lucky. This is true, not by chance though but by preparation for the right opportunity. For example, an aspiring music artist should always carry a copy of his or her demo and be prepared to perform at a moments notice.

I can remember when I wanted to be a singer as my father was a singer for an R&Bgroup. Well, he would take me to recording sessions, rehearsal sessions, and shows. I remember this one time that sticks with me, and probably one of the reasons I am not a singer today. My father knew I wanted to get into the industry, and he said: "I can walk you to the door and put the key in, but you have to turn the knob and walk in."

What he meant was he would set up the opportunity, but I needed to be prepared to utilize it. So at one of his shows, the crowd was huge and very excited, my father being the entertainer he is, managed to have everyone having a good time. He then out of nowhere said, "I want y'all to meet my son." Announced my name and called forme to come to the stage. I did not go I was not prepared for that opportunity. Aside from the regular crowd, there were also industry executives there.

See my father had the opportunity for me, yet I was not prepared. This was an example of not being prepared; in this case, I was not prepared to display my talent. I did not prepare myself to be able to perform at a moments notice or even to walk on stage. Two things came from that experience; my father has a great story to share at all his gatherings, and I learned first-hand to always be prepared for anything.

While these days I am far from being a singer, I still, however, also make sure I am prepared to present at the drop of a dime. I do not care what it is whether it is this book, my companies, or my daughter. I am always ready to present.

I remember not too long ago. Someone said what is "The Day Dreaming Mogul" and what do you stand for. On the spot, I gave an impromptu speech. This is because you never know whom you will come across. My mother used to tell me "Be careful how you treat strangers, you never know who is who."

This is very true, now she was referring to angels, stating that there could be a homeless person that could actually be an angel looking to test you for God. While I cannot confirm or deny people being angels, I will say that many people are walking the streets that can be very beneficial to your success and goals.

Nevertheless, as a general rule of thumb, I like to treat everyone as a client. This also is a way of being prepared, which is being prepared for a chance encounter.

So many stories come to mind in thinking of this. I can remember when I worked as a car salesman for a local dealership. The sales team that I worked with was excellent, I mean they could sell anything, but they were not always prepared. This one day that I will never forget, a gentleman came in with tattered, dirty clothes. No one wanted to greet the man. They prejudged him and discounted him by his appearance.

Well, I approached the gentleman, he told me he wanted to find an SUV. I took him out to the lot and conversed with the gentleman as I did with everyone. I told a few jokes and shared some things with him about me. This is what I did with all potential sales. It is a part of what I call taking the selling out of selling, it is very beneficial, yet I will save it for another book.

Anyway, I spent a good amount of time with the man, as I ran back and forth between the lot and the sales office getting different sets of keys for the man, I was stopped by a colleague. He said, "Nye, why are you wasting all this time with him?" I replied, "I do not look atit as wasting time, I am doing my job." They all laughed at me even the sales manager. It was OK, I continued with the man. I treated him as if he was from the DuPont family.

The gentleman left with out buying a vehicle. My sales team loved it and showed it with the laughter and jokes. I did not fret; I looked at it as an opportunity to sharpen my people skills. I honestly still felt good about my time with the gentleman. I figured even if he was homeless or whatever his story was, maybe treating him like everyone else made his day.

The next day the gentleman came back along with an older lady. He walked in; first, no one recognized him because he was dressed very differently. He was actually clean and nicely groomed. Everyone rushed to greet him. He smirked and asked me. I came out and noticed him because of his smile. He said he made his decision and wanted to do business today.

He walked outside and came back with the older lady. Well, the elderly lady was from the DuPont family, ironically. She explained the gentleman was the head of her grounds crew and she was tired of the station wagon that he drove around in so she demanded him to stop what he was doing and find a new car immediately. Which explained why he was dirty the day prior.

Because he told the lady about me and how he was impressed at the time and care I showed him. They did not haggle, and the bought a top of the line SUV at full list price. Oh and they bought the SUV in cash. I think that day everyone learned a lesson in being prepared and generally how to treat people. Surprisingly, I was the youngest person there but seemed to be the wisest. I was top salesman every month until I left.

As your daydream becomes more evident to you, you will be able to identify how you will need to be prepared. Your daydream will display luck, which is recognizing opportunities where your preparedness and opportunities will meet. I am not saying you will be clairvoyant. It is the power of your mind.

Once your daydream is set, and you are clear on what your goals are and what it takes to get there, your mind will run the scenario against your daily processes. Like a computer looking to crack a code, it will put together different combinations from what you do and think of day to day and what you hope to achieve.

CHAPTER EIGHT - LEARN SOMETHING NEW EVERYDAY

In the previous chapter, we talked about being prepared for opportunities. Part of being prepared is having knowledge. To effectively make your daydreams realities we must learn and be willing to learn everyday. Socrates said, "The only true wisdom is knowing that younker nothing." That is, we must have humble hearts and open minds. Remember that the mind operates off input and the more credible input that we provide our mind, the more vivid and viable our daydream will be hence, making them easier to transition to realities.

I remember when I was attempting to first start my record label. I used to go to a local record label called Ruff Nation. They were the label that released the "Fugees" and "Lauryn Hill". I was I think 17 at the time. I would journey up there everyday for like a week. I was prepared and preying on the opportunity. In other words, I was looking to get lucky.

I met a nice young lady by the name of Laiya. She was the receptionist at the time. She noticed what I was trying to do. When I say I was prepared, I mean I had CDs; I even had my artists waiting in the car in the event that the CD was not good enough. They would perform at the drop of a dime. Yet, I was not properly prepared in that according to Laiya, my presentation was not proper. Now because I keep an open mind and try to learn as much as I can. This was a great opportunity, she allowed me to pick her brain about what went on in the office. She told me with the way we were presented we would not be taken seriously.

With that information, we went home to properly prepare. We approached the next day with a proper presentation; I had one nicely dressed artist with me in the office and none in the car. I had a properly addressed package that contained the CD, bio, and pictures. The label did not pick us up but I did receive a phone call from the head of A&R for the label. He invited me to submit to him other demos or packages.

This was because I was open to learning the proper way of submitting a demo. If I did not listen to Laiya and her advice, I would not have even made it that far. The moral is while we want to be the most knowledgeable in the things we do, with an open mind we can learn how to enhance that knowledge be even more prepared.

Learning is not just the obtaining of knowledge; it is also exercising of the mind. My cousin, Darnell told me once "The more you know, the more interesting the world is. "I want to actually take that a step further. The more we learn the more variables are minds have to create solutions to problems, more possible combinations to crack our codes to success, and more scenarios to help with mapping our routes to success.

If you think of a daydream as a navigation system, navigation systems have to stay current with route updates, traffic, construction, accidents, etc. To do that we have to constantly up to date our units with DVDs, CD, the Internet, etc. Think of what would happen if your car had a GPS unit that was not current. We would be lost, stuck in traffic, and late to our destinations. The same applies to our minds and daydreams. If our minds are not updated with the latest information concerning our goals, dreams, and destinations, it could take us forever to reach them or even worse not reach them at all.

Where would you be as a carpenter if you only had hand tools and did not know of power tools? Going back to the Socrates quote, if you know that you know nothing, you would know that you have to learn and make that a priority. Daydreaming helps with learning as well, remember daydreaming is similar to watching a movie about what you are trying to do while your doing it. If we know what we need to learn about to achieve a goal we can be active in pursuing that knowledge and once we learn it we can actively put it in use. This allows us to understand it clearly by seeing it in action.

The beauty of the world that we live in now is that information is everywhere. There is nothing in the world that we cannot learn. This is thanks to Google, the Internet, etc. There are always books as well; there are books on everything. I am still amazed to this day at the variety of books that are readily available. When I was starting my Marketing Firm and Ad agency, I thought to myself where could I possibly find information on effectively starting an agency. When it dawned on me, I thought it was a voice in my head but it was actually mom's voice. What she said was so simple that was to pick up a book. So I went to the local bookstore and amazingly I found books on everything from how to find clients to hiring the right employee. Nevertheless, I found the right book and learned the ends and outs to start my firm.

Another great source of information is people. One of the best things you can do to understand about virtually anything is ask someone who does it. People love to talk especially about themselves I find the more successful they are the more they like to talk.

I know by now you can sense when I am about to go into a story. Well if you cannot tell, I do have a story to put this into perspective. When I was younger, my first job was working for my aunt Michele and her cleaning company. I was fourteen at the time. If you remember from a few chapters ago, I mentioned that I wanted to be an investment banker. Well, one particular Sunday evening I was cleaning an airport parking office. You know one of those places you park your car at while you fly.

Well anyway, I remember the valet pulled up a green Mercedes SL 600, that is the top of the line convertible for Mercedes. Well at the time, this was my favorite car. Breaking my attention from the car was the person receiving the keys. This guy had one of the sharpest suits that I have to this day ever seen. He looked as if he jumped right out of the movie "Wall Street." I was intrigued, being the type to never hold my tongue decided to approach this gentleman and ask what he did.

I was a scrawny fourteen-year-old kid who just finished cleaning a bathroom. I did not care, that man had information that I was determined to get. At the very least I would learn not to approach people or how to approach people.

I presented myself and greeted the gentleman in the most professional way I could. I introduced myself and complimented his car and suit. He smiled and thanked me, and then I went in for the kill. I said, "So what do you do for a living to have such nice things." The man laughed and said he was an investment banker for Morgan Stanley I believe. I was astounded; I knew it, so it began. I told him that was my dream job and proceeded to ask him what it was like and what it took to get there. The man did not have a problem sharing because he felt someone took an interest in what he did.

He probably was I at one point and had the same excitement about the career as I did. This could have reignited a love for his career. I say all of this to say if you come across people who may be somewhere you want to be or doing things you want to do, don't be afraid to ask. You can cut down years of research and get a true perspective of what you will be getting into.

Books are great, but they work better with a person who actually does these things because they are a working display of

the words in the book in action. The investment banker that I
met told me things that to this day I cannot find in books. This
is because in most cases books are mainly black and white.
People are the gray area. They are exceptions to rules, discoverer
ofshortcuts, etc.

The key to effectively daydreaming is again to ensure that your
mind has enough positive and credible input to paint the perfect
picture that guides you to each goal and ultimately achieving
success. In other words, your mind is the painter, and you are
the client looking for a great picture. The painter is not charging
you he just needs to be provided with the proper direction, tools,
motivations, paint, and a clean canvas that is large enough to fit
your picture.

These forms of learning are tools to build your vision in reality.
We can have everything in the world and all the opportunities
needed to be successful, yet if you do not have the proper tools
to maintain these things or be prepared for these opportunities,
we will not succeed.

Three men were walking along discussing their misfortunes
when one man came across a genie lamp. After rubbing the
lamp, a genie appeared. The genie told the men they had three
wishes to share. The first man thought about the misfortune in
his life and equated it to him being broke. He then asked the
genie for one million dollars. The genie granted it.

The man, not being used to such a sum of money spent it very
quickly and was right back where he started. Things were even
worse because the expenses were that of a person with one
million dollars income, not a lump sum.

The next man seeing this said that he was smarter than the
other man and asked for an enormous house with no mortgage.
He did not think about the taxes or insurance. The man's house
was severely damaged by a flood. He had no insurance, and he
could not afford the real estate taxes. The county in which he

lived seized the house.

The third man saw all of this and thought long and hard before he made his wish. The genie told him to be careful and mindful of his wish. The man's face lit up, he said: "genie, grant me with tools and knowledge." The genie was shocked, as he had never heard of such a wish. The man continued, "With the proper tools I can make as much money as I desire and if I lose it I can use the same tools to make it again. I can also buy whatever house I choose from the money made, and if I lose the house, I can use the tools and knowledge to buy another." The genie granted the wish, and the man did exactly as he said he would. He made millions of dollars and bought several houses that were adequately insured.

CHAPTER NINE - BE CAREFUL WHAT ASK FOR, YOU JUST MIGHT GET IT

In the previous chapter, we talked about being prepared for opportunities. Part of being prepared is having knowledge. To effectively make your daydreams realities we must learn and be willing to learn everyday. Socrates said, "The only true wisdom is knowing that younker nothing." That is, we must have humble hearts and open minds. Remember that the mind operates off input and the more credible input that we provide our mind, the more vivid and viable our daydream will be hence, making them easier to transition to realities.

You by now have realized the power of your mind, dreams, daydreams, and thought. I feel like I just handed the keys to a Ferrari with a full tank of gas to a person who just learned to drive. Like a Ferrari, your mind is fast and powerful. Yet, no matter how powerful, how expensive, and pretty it is, it should be correctly driven with caution.

Now I feel comfortable saying that you can do anything that you put your mind too. However, be cautious that your mind is the most efficient worker or tool you will ever see, meet, use, or employ. Understand that as soon as you lock your mind on what it is you want or think that you want. It will begin to work on putting it together.

Sometimes we do not think about what it is we want. We do

not look at or paint the whole picture. This is how we get in trouble. We again are not prepared for what we ask for.

A story that comes to mind when I think of this is about the starving children in Ethiopia. I remember being a child seeing the commercial that asked for donations to feed them. Well, watching this one day in my childhood ignorance and lack of understanding I smirked and said that was stupid. My mother asked me what I was talking about. I told her that the all we had to do was send a whole bunch of McDonald's food and Thanksgiving dinner and they should be full and no longer hungry. My mom sat me down and explained that a person who has not eaten in a long time, well their body would not be able to correctly handle and digest the food. She also said that large portions could possibly kill the people.

The moral that I take from this story is that while it may seem that solutions, needs, or wants may be right there. However, not being prepared for that opportunity could prove to cause more harm than help. As I became older, I have seen this example increasingly. One of the main things that people wish for is to hit the lottery or come into a windfall of cash. The problem is lack of preparedness. Most people who win lotteries, major lawsuits, get inheritances, etc. lose their windfalls in a year or less.

This loss is because they are not prepared for what they asked. The full picture is not painted that includes the negatives and positives of what they ask.

Another story that demonstrates this principle is one of a business owner client of my marketing firm. This client owned a service company, providing services to businesses and the public. They were stuck in a rut so to speak, in that; they had the same cycle of business. They were comfortable with the same revenue, profit, etc. Well, they wanted to expand and make more. The owner thought that the key to this would be marketing.

In this particular case, I was able to take them from being exposed to a potential market of 10,000 to 188,000 with the marketing plans and campaigns I created. The man thought of the revenue this would create and he got excited. As a courtesy, I advised my client that he should ensure that he was prepared for the dramatic change this would cause. He insisted the company would fair well and comfortably adapt to the influx of customers and demand for service.

The problem was his thought process was still on the way his business had been for years prior. He looked solely at the change in income but not what it would take to efficiently facilitate such new demand and request. We executed the campaign, and as planned, the customers came calling.

I remember making a visit to check on my client, and he had not slept in a week. He told me that his people were not used to that much work and some of them quit. Eventually, his company adapted to the demand, and they were OK but at the cost of his health, his personal relationship, and the providing of quality service. I heard he and his wife had problems because of the strain the business put on his home life, as he was never home.

As a result, to the stress of home and work, he had a heart attack, and due to the company having just too many clients and not enough employees, the quality of the service suffered. It sounded perfect to have exposure to over 188,000 people when he was used 10,000. However, he did not realize or consider that is several times the exposure that his company was a custom to having. This meant that virtually everything needed to be multiplied.

He learned a valuable lesson as did I and I hope you will. By all means, we should dream big but dream the whole picture. To ensure that we are prepared we should ask ourselves a few questions when assessing our goals. That is, how will accomplishing this goal change the way I live my life now? How will it affect the people in my life? What do I need or what should I do to accommodate these changes? These are just a few questions just to give you an idea of what you should be thinking about when daydreaming. Much like daydreaming this principle applies to anything that you wish for or aspire to obtain, no matter what aspect of your life it concerns.

CHAPTER TEN - IT'S YOUR DREAM, ACT LIKE IT

Now you have the basic of daydreaming and utilizing it to guide you to your goals. All you have to do now is go out and do it. I do not mean just plan your goals out and start daydreaming about it. I propose you begin dreaming and acting out your dreams by day with open eyes.

In my life and business, I get the privilege of meeting so many creative, intelligent, and all around great people. I see them and wonder why are they not doing what they love; why are they so unhappy, or why do they not realize what they are capable. Most of us are acting out a dream, the problem is, that it is not ours. It is someone else's whether it is a boss or owner of the company you work for or a relationship in your life whether it is with a parent, child, lover, husband, wife, etc.

I want to take a little time and explore this with you. This is important to me, and it is a realization that could make your life more fruitful. It is a cold realization at first, but I mean no harm. The sooner you realize this, the sooner you start to correct it.

I stated that most of us are acting out someone else's dream. Let us first visit the career aspect of this. Now I do not care what your career is whether it is entry level or executive level. If you are not the majority shareholder, partner, member or sole proprietor of the organization, you are acting out someone's dream. This is not necessarily a bad thing.

I have some friends who are executives and are happy. This is because while they have major responsibilities, they do not have as much as the owner or the lead person for the organization. In fact, while they do not own their organization, in some cases they make more money than people who do. The key is to clearly understand where you are so you can identify and determine where you are going.

On the other hand, if you are working at an organization with hopes and dreams of having your own or being somewhere else. Sometimes you feel like you may be spinning your wheels because you may not have made that realization. Daydreaming will assist you. First, you must change from being just a part of someone else's dream of making it a part of yours.

What I mean is figure out how the skills that you utilize or money that you make can aid you in doing what you wish to do or accomplish. I look at working for companies asextended learning. Each day I would go into to my employer no matter who it was, the car dealership, my aunt's company, or the banks. You should at the very least be able to understand key business models from where you work.

You look puzzled, think about it. Every business is in business to make money. Look at what that organization does to make money. Every business operates on the same two key functions, that is supply and demand and revenue minus expenses equals profit. The rest is just plugging your life into that model. Whether you want to start your own business or progress in the company in which you are currently employed. I guarantee if you understand thesethings you will become more efficient. This is because you will begin to daydream about these processes and either how to make them better, how to become a more proficient element, or how to apply it to your goals.

Now the key is to figure out what to do with what you gain through this process. Again these statements aren't meant to be negative or to cause mutiny at work. It is to understand what makes the world go around. The truth is all of our dream interweavings with each other make the world go around. Do not feel defeatist about your situation.

Look at it as a partnership; you are helping someone achieve his or her goals and dreams. It only feels one-sided right now because you have not realized how they are helping you with yours. Have you ever worked anywhere that says, "You will work here, but you cannot learn from our organization?" No that is absurd. Most of us do not realize or look at our jobs and careers as a learning opportunity. We look at it as work, and unfortunately, we have developed a negative implication of the word. So, if you feel bad about work or what you do, do not. Daydream and realize what your partnership offers and utilize it.

Now on to the relationship part of the statement, I indicated that if you are in a relationship, you are part of someone else's dream. It should be a wonderful feeling to feel that you are apart of someone else's dream. I love to think that I make someone happy and are in their thoughts. The problem is that too often, in relationships people feel that they are not enough for the other person or someone is not doing enough to make it work. This is mainly because people forget about the partnership aspect of the relationship.

This is very broad and can be applied to all relationships, friends, parent and child, siblings, lovers, etc. Because for any of these relationships to work the chief component is the same, communication, empathy, thoughtfulness, companionship, and affection.

Daydreaming can be used to ensure strength in and achieving successful relationships. As I indicated earlier daydreaming doesnot solely apply to achieving wealth, material,status, fame, etc. It applies to everything you care about and think about. The mind again has a key part to play in the success applying daydreaming to the relationship. The difference is in this partnership, each party must also be mindful of the others input. That is watching what you say, do, and how you act towards the other member of your relationship.

If in your relationship you never show appreciation for the other person in the relationship. They never have input that would lead them to believe that they are appreciated. Most of us need to feel appreciated, and when we do not get it from somewhere, we seek it elsewhere or began to self-destruct. It

Is still the same mental fundamentals of everything else, input, process and calculation, and output. Garbage in garbage out also applies. If we have negative input, our minds process it and turn everything having to do with that situation negative, which in turns causes negative output. Unfortunately, the list of negative output is very long, but they all hurt.

That then becomes the goal to hurt as retaliation or defense. What people more common than not forgetis that we are all equal. It does not matter what you bring to a relationship or the type of relationship. You are in that person's life for more than likely that same reason they are in yours.

There is naturally a few exceptions namely family. In non-family relationships, however, it does not matter who has what material, physically, mentally, or emotionally. That fact remains that you are partners. The sooner people realize this, the sooner relationships become healthier.

I am not saying there will not be problems in the relationship.I am saying to treat the problems and that person as you would treat yourself. It is all summed up as in the golden rule. This you can apply to family relationships as well. I had to realize that while my mom is the superwoman in my life, she has feelings too that can be hurt. She too needs to know she is appreciated. Parents are a special case.

Most parents dream to make sure their children have great lives and go on to accomplish whatever they want. They need input to process as well no matter how old or transcendent they are. I ran into a problem with my mother that stemmed from communication.

She had her daydreams for me but with no updates. I only would call her if I had problems. This made her disconnect from me so to speak. Her mind began to process that the only time I would call is when I needed something. This caused her pain, so her mind concocted a solution, and the output was to stop interacting with me.

This was an explicit example of my life of a problem caused when I took for granted my mother's mental process and the equality of our relationship. I am pleased to say thatwe have reconciled our differences. This came from the same understanding of not just each other's feeling but our minds.

Just as children need a sign of approval from parents, the reciprocal is parents need to a sign of appreciation and acknowledgment that we realize what all they do and sacrifice for us. Every relationship you have should enhance your life. I believe that also every relationship in your life should enhance your daydream as you should enhance the other person's daydream as well.

Imagine how much easier it would be to achieve goals and success with someone in your corner who shares and supports your vision. Think of your favorite movie, sure there is a leading actor, but he or she has a supporting cast. Together they enhance each other's performance. Identify your supporting cast but also remember that everyone you identify, you should distinguish how you fit in as a member of their supporting cast. Remember relationships are about equality and they work efficiently by communication.

Your dreams and daydreams are your movies; they can be romantic movies, dramas, comedies, etc. Just as in any successful film there needs to be proper direction, which is accomplished by appropriate and effective communication. Communicate with the supporting cast of your life. Let them know what you are doing and how they fit. They can be a very positive source of input for your mind and daydreams as you can be for theirs. Your most valuable network could be the one that you already have around you. It does not matter what your goals or dreams consist of. However, you will never know unless you ask or take a genuine interest in what your friends and family are involved in.

The great thing about your supporting cast is, they will support you in what you do, which generally means that they will make the things you are trying to do much easier than attempting to deal with strangers.

Here is an example; let's assume that you want to start a business. For the sake of the example, let's assume you are starting a general service company. In any case, you already have a business plan and your business license. Now you need to find clients by way of flyers, business cards, and maybe even a website. Being that you are a start-up company you do not have a significant budget.

One day you go to a friends house and notice that he or she is doodling on the computer and created some exceptional images and graphics. Is it making sense where I'm going now? Remember, your daydream is allowing you to filter in the things in your surroundings that would help to achieve. You have a designer there to create your business cards, flyers, etc. Because this is your friend, more than likely they either will not charge you, or charge you a minimal fee.

Do not feel like you are using them, this is a balanced

situation. By you asking for help, it displays your interest in what your friends are doing also showing your confidence in their craft. You can even in return possibly inspire that person to start his or her own business. You could be their first client and also advertise for them.

This is an example of how just a little awareness and acknowledgment of your supporting cast can assist you and save your time and money. Of course, the talents and abilities are not limited to those in this example. It is up to you to realize who is in your supporting cast how you can support each other.

Now that you realize your ability to daydream and the importance of your supporting cast. The final step is acting out your dreams. While daydreaming can be entertaining and get you through the day, to efficiently utilize this tool you have to act it out. Your mind will only do so much, it's still on you to do the things displayed in your mind and dreams. You have to act as if you are on screen looking to win an award. Believe in what you are daydreaming and follow the blueprint. Think of it this way, what good is a book full of knowledge if you do not practice you're learning. For that matter, what good is this book if you do not practice the contents and apply them to your life.

CHAPTER ELEVEN - FEAR AND THE FINAL WORD, SUCCESS

Many of us are limited by our own fears. Ironic as it may sound, the biggest fears are the fears of our own successes and failures. I like to think that if I can realize I failed I have succeeded. That is realizing failure means that I have succeeded in learning what went wrong, what to or not to do, etc. I too had both of these fears, but it was not until I realized this notion that I was able to overcome these fears.

There is a saying that comes to mind when trying to explain this, that is, "A man to fear is a man with nothing to lose." I know this sounds a little extreme when trying to express a positive point. This saying is normally applied to a negative circumstance. Yet, I want you to think of it positively to help you overcome the said fear.

If you regard every situation as having nothing to lose you will be less reluctant to try or to go after your dreams and goals. Do not think about the possibility of failure because failure at the very least is a learning opportunity. Therefore, you have nothing to lose but all to gain.

You are a person to fear because you will go after what it is that you desire. Success again is defined by the person who uses the word. It is important that when you relate said success to your goals, its definition is consistent throughout the entire process. When you initially daydream about what you want or need. Determine your definition of success at that point. Each goal set should align with a path to reach your definition or determination of success. Ensure that the primary input that you surround yourself with has the same theme of your success. This is important in not losing your focus or your mind losing focus and being sidetracked.

Your mind will pick up on all the things that aid in your success. If you are not consistent in that definition, well your mind will begin to clutter with things that it determines you need or want. This leads to people becoming easily sidetracked. We want our minds to be clear and efficiently guide us to our goals.

The fear of success is a little different. It is just as bad as the fear of failure if not worse. The fear of success limits a person and causes them to sabotage themselves. The biggest element in a success that causes this fear is change. It is human nature to be uncomfortable with change. We get used to our normal cycles in life, and when we introduce a change in our routines, we interrupt our comfort zones.

This fear is dangerous because it is misleading and somewhat hidden. Fear of failure may not allow you to go after your goals and dreams, while fear of success, will allow you to start. The fear of success will cause you to waste time and possibly money. It may also cause one to lose credibility among your peer, friends, and associates.

Here is an example; let's assume you are going after a major promotion at your job. You have seemingly set in your mind that this is what you want to do and have realized that you can and will achieve this goal. Unbeknownst to you, you have a fear of success. You began to let everyone know that you are going

48

to apply for this promotion including your superiors at work. You explained and began to show that you are serious and started taking on extra responsibilities, learning all about your future position and talking as if you are entirely up to the task.

Then it happens, the fear causes you to began to sabotage yourself. You started making errors that are thoughtless and entirely out of your character. It is almost as if you have pushed an internal self-destruct button. What happens now? Not only do you lose the promotion, but you lose credibility of your superiors and peers. People will begin to think that you talk a good game but are full of it so to speak. In some situations, depending onhow bad the errors you could lose your job.

I know this sounds kinda scary, however, unfortunately, this happens every day. You may be wondering how to overcome such a deadly fear. Well, it is simple, you must create a comfort zone for the reality that you are aiming to experience. The solution to do this is honestly, daydreaming. By now you should see how this can be a solution to the problem; however, I will explain.

Discomfort comes from unfamiliarity. In the example mentioned above, you may have dreamed of the position you were going for, yet these were dreams that occurred in your subconscious. So your consciousness had now an idea of the potential reality of your promotion, or taking steps to get there. Therefore, when you actually began putting these actions to play, your mind was not ready, and everything was somewhat new to you.

Think of it as if you were not active, like a couch potato and you decided one day that you wanted to run a marathon. You have not trained or even ran a long distance in years for that matter. What would happen? Well, you may possibly do significant damage to your body, and you definitely would not finish the marathon. Your body was not ready for such a dramatic change. This means we have to prepare for any significant transformation in our lives, physically, mentally, or emotionally.

Daydreaming allows you to condition for such changes. Let's assume in the previous job promotion example that you daydreamed about this. Remember, daydreaming is like a movie playing in your mind while you are conscious and can be utilized in any setting. So, while you are at work, you are daydreaming about the position that you are going after. You know exactly what you have to do to obtain it. So your mind puts things together that allow you to become comfortable with your task and the changes before they happen. So your fear of success has no chance to sabotage you because you are already comfortable. It is almost as if you have been doing these new things the whole time. Everything seems familiar, sort of like "Deja vu." Remember it is all in your mind, fear, success, joy, pain, etc. Therefore, if our mind is conditioned and we harness the power and control our minds.

We can literally overcome anything and be successful at everything. So daydream, take the time to define your success, and give your all. Remember, the worst that happens if you fail, which is still a victory for you. You will learn from your errors,provide more input for your mind and you will also develop resiliency.

PART II - CREDIT SCORE DATING
THE SEXINESS OF CREDIT

INTRODUCTION

In life two things will forever be in demand and forever depend on each other, they are relationships and finance. It doesn't matter what type of relationship, working, personal, or family, they all at some point or consistently involve and sometimes dissolve because of finance.

Hello, again all it has been a while since I've had the pleasure of writing for you all. I'm Niem M. Green, CEO of the Creditscoredating.com, also referred to as "The Daydreaming Mogul." Now for my fans and readers from the first book in the series "The Daydreaming Mogul's Guide Vol. 1 Daydreams and Success" that I like to lay out a few disclosures before we get started. This time I'd like to do the same. However, it is a little different as I am as some would call a subject matter expert in the topic we will discuss in this book. While I've created the algorithm and trade secret behind the revolutionary site "Creditscoredating.com" that is matching singles up by credit and financial compatibility, I am not a psychologist or psychiatrist for that matter. I am, however, a career trained credit analyst and underwriter. I have made decisions on countless credit applications over 15 years from mortgage loans to credit cards and everything in between.

I also have brought a friend along with me this time. I'd like to introduce Kier A. Berkel, NCC, LPCMH, a Licensed Psychotherapist with a practice in New Castle, Delaware.

While Kier specializes in many things, he has years of experience in relationship and marital experiences. Together we will offer an interactive and experienced look at credit score dating. He speaks from a therapeutic point of view and me from more of an analytical approach.

I own Creditscoredating.com, and we match singles by their credit among other things. Sounds crazy right? Well maybe not so much, this is what I will discuss with you in this book. Our company's tagline is "Where Good Credit is Sexy" ™, this is what we will explore the "sexiness" of credit. I know some of you are thinking "how in the world is credit sexy?" No worries, I have received that same response from countless reporters, talk show hosts, and the general public all over the world.

So let us get into this, shall we? Back to the opening statement, sometimes relationships dissolve because of finance. In fact, the leading cause of divorce and relationship turmoil has been financial or monetary issues. At the bank as an underwriter, my job in its simplest terms was to determine the relationship with the potential borrower. In fact, in many cases, this determination is made in 90 seconds or less. In essence, as an underwriter, I was a matchmaker. I had to determine the likelihood of "divorce" or default if we were to extend credit to that borrower. In personal relationships, singles date to find that "right one." Through the courting or dating process, they determine the likelihood of "default" or divorce.

Isn't this interesting? Did you know that while you were dating, you were underwriting to approve or deny your love or time? Hold on, because we barely scratched the surface. By the end of this book, you will be equipped with a more refined knowledge of credit and its importance in life and relationships. You will also be what I like to call "relationship underwriters." Even if you are currently in a relationship, dating, or considering it, you will be equipped to look at things from a more analytical point of view which will help to better your odds at success in your relationships.

My goal is not to scare you from taking risks but to help you to understand that tools to better calculate said risks. It is also imperative that I clarify that wanting good credit or a mate with good credit does not make you "gold digger." We will talk about this further in later chapters; I will say this, in hundreds of thousands, possibly millions of applications and credit reports I've analyzed, I've noticed that some people with higher scores had lower incomes than those with higher incomes. It appeared that people with lower incomes with good credit were conditioned to spend and budget within and below their means. The people with higher incomes seemed to live above and have a higher reliance on credit. Again, we will discuss this further in later in this book.

The goal of this book much like my dating site is to educate. While I may be accredited from my degree, my experience in lending, and even my website. I want you all to take this advice and my accreditation into consideration, not as a businessman and public figure who has spoken throughout the world or been on major news and TV globally. Just as a fellow consumer who has had bad credit and good, great relationships and horrible relationships. The thing in common about both situations regarding credit and relationships is the ignorance, that is, lack of information and knowledge. My losses become your gains; my failures become your successes with this book.

Strap on your seat-belts and prepare to be educated and entertained on this rollercoaster ride of love and credit and credit score dating, "where good credit is sexy." ™ Because "It All Starts with a Number." ™

CHAPTER 1 - INITIAL FEELING

You've been looking for the perfect match, you've heard your friends, family, and co-workers talking about it. This love interest may be your first time; maybe you've had others. Possibly the last relationships ended terribly; perhaps they ended on more favorable terms. Nonetheless, you're starting to give up, in fact, people are telling you, "you can't look for it, it'll happen when you stop looking." You think, "that's easy to say when you have found your perfect match." Licensed Psychotherapist, Kier A. Berkel of New Castle, DE simplifies this as "People need people."

Finally, it happens, you meet someone that seems to satisfy everything in your criteria. They answered every question right; they had the right tone, their approach was correct. It is that "Initial Feeling," you're enamored. You think that this must be what you've been waiting for the entire time. This person was made just for you. They are the perfect match.

This sense is the initial feeling that we felt as underwriters also, "Oh yeah, they're approved." Their application looks correct, their credit report looks good, their credit score fit within the approvable guidelines, and they answered everything just right. However, we could have been wrong, much like in meeting someone new. A new applicant for credit is much like a new applicant for courtship. We often put our best foot forward when meeting new people, especially when something we want is on the line. We're taught at an early age that "first impressions are everything."

"We don't have to be taught to want to socialize; it's usually innate. If we have a good upbringing, when we're born, if we have that nurturing that we need it's already preprogrammed in us to be social creatures. So it's nothing that we have to think about, although we make it complicated, it is naturally within us." - Kier

My co-workers and I used to call some of these applicants "career applicants." They would go from bank to bank to study application processes to find out what questions asked and what the application processes would be, that is how strenuous or how easy the applications were.

These applicants were easy to spot after a while; they seemed too good to be true. They knew the right answers; they knew bank jargon even. They would also cite acronyms that I would otherwise only hear in the bank.

While it is true that a percentage of this applicant may have been versed in the process, and possibly may even have had lending backgrounds, the majority had not. How did we know the difference? What was the telltale? Their credit file didn't add up. For example, why were they on the phone with me in the first place? Well, typically if you find yourself on the phone with an underwriter for a credit card, it is for one of two reasons, either verification, something needs confirmation; address, phone, etc. or they need clarification of something credit related.

The other telltale was the number of inquiries from credit card companies in one period. If there are many at one time, it is possible that it is fraud. However, that is an entirely different "talk show," so I'll save that for another book and time.

Now how does this relate to dating? I'm sure you're wondering. Have you ever met someone and they seem to be perfect and answer everything correctly, yet something just doesn't add up? Let's apply the same credit applicant to a dating scenario.

The suitor, man or woman, is perfect, from their personality to their smile. They answer all of your questions correctly, almost as if they've practiced the night before. (They probably have, just on a different person, ok, ok I'll hold my cynicism.) However, you start to talk about their past relationships or dating experiences. Could be later that evening or on another date, and they tell you a long list of people who it didn't work. It could be just the last relationship they were in that it did not work. Nonetheless, it is 1 of 2 things, the other person's fault or "mutually they've decided it separate on good terms."

This person is what we'll call a "career dater," they've found the sweet spot how they can best answer the question that everyone seems to get "You're so great, why are you single?" without looking bad.

Think of that episode of Seinfeld, when George used the picture of Jerry's girlfriend along with the story that his ex-fiancé died. This scenario is the same philosophy, of course, the show used the comical approach, nevertheless, career daters try to find the correct answers and group of circumstances that will incite the interest of the person they're trying to date.

I joined Dagen Mcdowell of Fox Business News and Fox News, for a news segment in which she stated;

"I can tell you how you can identify this without, no offense to Niem, without using his service. If you go out with a guy and he spends a lot of money on your very first date, that is a troubling sign, Or if the person dresses in a way that is too expensive for the job he has." - Dagen Mcdowell

One thing I will say that I've learned over the years is not to cast judgment. I am however analytical by nature and by trade. With that being said, I'm sure it is possible that there are people out there who somehow to manage to date a lot without wrongdoing. However, what are those odds? Seriously, those would have to be minimal odds.

We are imperfect; I am no exception, I'm sure there are a few people who would tend to agree. With our imperfections and being creatures of habit, it takes a few tries sometimes to get things correct. Relationships and dating are no exception. You can't appreciate the best if you've never experienced the worst. We can't perfect something without making mistakes. Hence, the saying "practice makes perfect." Dating and relationships are no exception; we have to learn and grow individually as well as in relationships to perfect our interpersonal interaction, skill, and competencies.

If there were this "perfect" flawless person out there with a 100% dating percentage, I'm almost certain they are in a serious relationship or married. Even Beyoncé, who made the song "Flawless" is married.

I took a bit of a lighthearted approach to the matter just to break the ice. The point is still the same, however, and to remember is the "initial feeling." While yes, the initial feeling is a great one, the key to keeping the relationship fresh is to recreate the initial feeling. Be cautioned that there is another initial feeling that we sometimes do not pay attention to or take heed that is one of caution and risk factors. "If it seems to good to be true, it probably is." This saying is an old saying that is passed from parent to child amongst families and generations for a good reason.

Sometimes not taking heed to cautionary "initial feeling" is like approving a bad loan. The one thing in underwriting that is worse than approving a bad loan is not asking the proper questions to prevent from approving a bad loan.

Bad loans happen, that's a part of life and part of the lending world and environment. As in relationships, there will be breakups and bad relationships, that is a part of life. Again, this is a part of our growth, maturity, and learning how to manage our relationships. Many variables and forces affect both, loans and relationships. We will touch on this in a later chapter, however, worse than being in a bad relationship is not trying to prevent it.

Would you purposely put yourself in the worst situation ever? Of course not, yet this is what we do when we do not take heed of the initial cautionary feeling.

At the bank, I would see other underwriters try to meet their goals of approval rates by not doing illegal things but by not paying attention to their cautionary "initial feelings." What would happen is that their approval rates would be high but their legacy, or accounts that they've approved over time, default rates would become higher. The result became the same, and it was never good for the bank, the borrower, or the underwriter.

Applying this to relationships, if we just look at the "glittering" of being in a relationship and not pay attention to the initial cautionary feeling and take the time to understand why it is there and investigate, the result is often the same. One or both people in the relationship are hurt and unfortunately, if there are children involved they are also hurt. Often after relationships suffer and turn for the worst, the parties typically say, "I never knew he or she was like that, it was like they turn into a different person." The signs were there the entire time. In a lot of cases, we tend to turn a blind eye to these things or ignore the cautionary "initial feeling" because of what we want or what we feel we "need." We "need" to be with someone, we "need" to find a wife or husband, we don't "need" to sleep alone anymore. Our kids "need" a mother or father, we "need" to have kids, etc. Much like my fellow underwriters, they "need" to hit their approval goals, the "need" to get their bonuses, etc. There is every incentive to overlook the initial cautionary feeling for the good initial feeling.

Another old saying, "haste makes waste" my mother and grandmother, used to say this to me all the time. This can indeed be applied here also in both scenarios. If we hastily rush to make decisions, jump in a relationship, make approvals, etc. what do we end up with? We waste our time, our careers in some cases, end up with broken hearts, etc.

Part of the blame still lies on us also, by looking at what we feel without evaluating our strengths or weaknesses. In some cases, we know we ignore this. I'm not talking about the superficial or surface things. Sure that beautiful person is compatible with us on "paper." You may even have the best photos ever and can imagine the cute baby together. However, what about this person matching with you on the worst day? How do they react to some of your flaws, behaviors, or whatever things you may not readily admit to others?

My aunt used to prepare me financially for things I wanted. She would say, "Yeah, you have money and in your account, so things look easy to afford. But what about that bad day when there's an unexpected expense of even became too excited and overspent? Can you afford it? If you can afford it on your worst day in the worst circumstances, then go ahead and buy it."

My Aunt Michelle will tell you, I didn't always listen, and it took a while to catch on. This failure isn't because of any disability; it's merely I am human and the "initial feeling" caught me several times.

There is an excellent value in this, and it can be applied to relationships also. Think of all you know of the person you're with and the worst scenario you experienced. Granted, some of you are in relationships and may have been through bad experiences. How did you and your mate fair? Did this cause a disturbance in your relationship or life? If you aren't in a relationship or haven't experienced any issues similar to what I'm describing, how do you think the person you are dating or considering will manage? Do you feel there are some signs in them or you that will conflict or escalate an already bad situation?

In some cases, we assess certain things about a person and say, "yeah, I can change or they will." What happens if you can't or they won't? Remember, we are looking at the worst scenario and placing this person in it. With that said, stress and pressure have a habit of changing people. So if typically a person would be receptive to your requests, comments, criticism, etc. the stress may cause a different response.

This example all goes back to paying attention to both "Initial Feelings." The same is true for us in underwriting. In some cases, we have to look to see if an applicant would be approvable in a certain situation. This situation could be good or bad; it could be our approval would have broken them and turned them into a risk. I will talk more about this later. We see why it's important to pay attention to what "Initial Feeling" is stronger and investigate why it is there.

"People research the car they want. But they don't look at the back end of it, they look on the surface but don't look in depth at their purchase. Similarly, in dating people look at the looks and personality, everything at a surface level. But as the relationship develops and becomes more serious, the learn who this person is at the wrong times. Like when buying a car and were expecting their partner was compatible with them financially, but they weren't. They feel deceived, it's risky. This situation is why people need to take that step and precautions to make sure they know who they are dating is compatible with them financially." - Sean Johnson, General Manager, Porsche Delaware

"We want to exaggerate that image that the person has already perceived. Let's think of a young lady who's graduating from high school. She's getting notice; she's getting attention. Her foundation is telling her, "a man is not going to want you if you don't act like a lady, you have to act feminine. If you like sports that's cool but play that down a little bit, because that's not what a man is looking for." Same thing for men, "you've got to be masculine about it. Grow some facial hair, wear Timberlands you know, engage yourself in things society thinks are masculine." We don't teach the younger generations about being themselves. It's all about getting that man or that woman, getting that application, or getting that deal. So that's where the deception comes from in my opinion because we are brought up with these perceptions that are just lies. We carry it throughout our lives into our dating world, into our career world, all of these perceived ideas of what people want." - Kier Berkel

CHAPTER 2 - NEW ERA OF DATING

This world is a new world of everything; it is a time of advanced technology. We have the entire world in our hands. However, this is also a time of what Kier calls "instant gratification," a time when everyone wants what they want when they want it. That time is often now, "not now, but right now." This is for purchases, big or small, one time or recurring, careers, and even relationships.

It is hard to imagine there was a time that a person had to wait up to a minute to connect to the internet using dial-up. I can still remember the sound of the modem dialing into AOL. My daughter often laughs at me when I tell her stories of this and other things that seem like impossibilities to her. Just as to me it is hard to imagine there was a time when to speak with a loved one across the country or world, you would have to wait weeks, months, or years.

Try telling a jealous girlfriend that one, "Hey babe, I'll be back, but I'll write you, so you'll hear from me every 6 - 12 months." With the right or wrong girlfriend or significant other more than likely, you would not leave, or you would not go alone.

This scenario poses a good question, jealousy in relationships, has technology influenced this or has does it help with this? Is there just cause for this or does it add to the high relationship turnover rates? With the rise of social networks, the world seems to be a buffet of "selfies," personal or overstated information, etc. Frivolous relationships seem to be on the rise and fall (breakups) also, and the world knows about it all, thanks to social media and camera phones.

This seems to be the new way of relationships;

Like a picture on a random social media site

Post a witty comment or two with a cute emoji

Direct message your number

Text a simple "WYD" (What You Doing)

Arrange time to meet for casual date

Eventually, have sex

Argue followed by break up

Like a new picture and repeat process

Now, this may be a little extreme, and I pray I didn't just describe your routine and if I did, please find a new one. However, this is where we seem to be, quick relationships that lack substance. I grew up with meeting people online as a teenager, which was exciting. This may be part of why I developed an interest in the online dating business.

Online dating is not a bad thing, in fact, online dating is great especially for those with busy schedules or those who don't wish to meet people in bars and other places. I also say that online dating allows for singles to connect with and become attracted to a person's personality. Quickly we move past just seeing someone's profile picture and actuate into learning about their mind or character.

Some people have different complexes, fears, and inabilities that prohibit them from showing their true self in an offline environment. While yes, some people take the online approach too far, I.e. "Catfishing" and other forms of deception and false personas. There are many people who genuinely find online dating as a haven and place to be and display "themselves" and hope to meet people to accept them for who they are.

Similarly, car buyers have used these advancements to make care purchases. Cars are typically the second most significant purchase for the average consumer.

"Car buyers come in as I call them "prepared." They know exactly what they want with all the specifications and price of the car before they meet with me." - Brandon Rogers of Porsche Delaware

Brandon has years of experience as a sales consultant and has seen it all.

"The buyers want what they want when they want it. They know everything about the color to the options they want. The only thing left is the price, that is what they meet with us about, essentially the car is sold before I first greet them." - Brandon Rogers

This again from the technological advancement allowing for customers to become "prepared."

There used to be a stigma of dating online, however, studies show that that stigma has and continues to fade away. In fact, online dating has become part of pop culture. According to Pew Research Center, in 2005 44% of Americans agreed that online dating is an excellent way to meet people. In 2013 the percentage increased to 59%. My thought is that this correlates with the advancement and greater access to technology. I believe that this corresponds to Kier's theory of instant gratification and my idea of connecting with people's personalities while maintaining busy schedules.

If you look at some of the popular social networks and how they are used, people are posting their lives, thoughts, feelings, views, etc. almost to a fault without demarcation. This use makes it easier to connect with others without reservation and create a profile on an online dating site.

While the methods of connecting and meeting people may have changed or advanced, the problems of dating, relationships, and marriage have not. Relationships still end every day, people are nevertheless filing for divorce, and singles still have reservations, fears, complexes, insecurities, etc. about relationships, dating, and committing. Money is still "the leading cause of stress in relationships" according to CNBC in a report published February 2015.

With all the technological advances, why have we not advanced as humans and singles to solve the money problem? What would be that solution? As I mentioned earlier in the introduction, my background was underwriting and analyst for banks. I also stated that I am the CEO of CreditScoreDating. com. I have and continue to refine the algorithm to address this question and find the solution. However, the resolution, I've discovered over the years of running the site and working for various banks is straightforward.

The funny thing is, you don't have to be a data engineer, underwriter, or risk analyst to find the solution. The solution, much like most solutions in relationships, whether romantic, friendships, business, etc. lies in communication.

While my algorithm and site can and is designed to match singles by financial wherewithal and compatibility, the primary goal is to get singles to discuss what they never consider until it is too late, the leading cause of relationship stress and divorce, finance.

A lot of times, especially in the beginning of relationships, we talk and communicate. It's an exciting time, whether we are chatting with someone online, spending hours talking on the phone or texting throughout the day.

We want to know about this person; we love their voice, their laugh, their jokes, etc. We also want them to know about us. Ironically we often leave out the most important things that will determine the length or possibility of success in our relationships.

Let me make the disclosure that I'm not talking about if you are not dating seriously or your goal is for "one night love," as my friends and I call it. This, much like the rest of this book and my website is for serious relationships.

Sometimes, however, we do get caught up in the physical, sexual, or mental attractions that we don't want to find reasons to end. This goes back to the previous chapter and the "initial feeling."

With the advancement of technology, there is every temptation to ignore the initial cautionary feeling. Yes, there is a lot of lures with easier access thanks to these improvements, but we are focusing on this one in particular.

With us putting so much of ourselves online, in all forms. We have more incentives to ignore our initial cautionary feelings. Whether it is because that person has lips that are so kissable, we can't wait to feel them, or they seem like the perfect yin to our yang, based on responses, posts, etc. you've observed.

Just as Brandon explained with car buying, people are "prepared" in online dating from the profiles information, posts, likes, etc. They know about their potential mate before the first, "Hey, WYD (What you doing?) message comes through.

I'm not exempt from this; I'm human. Therefore I couldn't possibly say, "Don't do this, don't do that." I would be a hypocrite, in fact, I love the advancement of technology and appreciative of all it's done for me personally and in my career and business. I'm simply offering my advice to be cautious and know what we are up against when it comes to relationships and finding the correct person for us to be happy.

CHAPTER 3 - 'TIL DEBT DO US PART

"Til' Debt Do Us Part" I know it seems like this would be the last chapter in a relationship book. I want to approach this from an analytical approach. As an underwriter at the bank, I have trained that credit was the first step of collections. The better job we do underwriting, the easier job it would be for the collectors in the event the account went bad. The goal, however, was to ensure we did not approve an account that would not go bad. In relationships the better job we do at looking at what causes failure, the more effective we can be a success.

I mentioned that one of the main reasons that relationships fail is finance and the leading cause of relationship stress is finance. That is very vague, in fact, the topic of finance is very ambiguous.

In my career owning the site, from Creditscoredating.com to being an underwriter, I've heard it all. From spouses and significant others with spending problems to just not paying bills. However, one of the greatest financial issues plaguing relationships is "Debt."

According to the Fair Issac Corporation, the company that issues the FICO score, debt makes up 30% of the FICO score calculation. Debt is only second to payment history, which makes up 35% of the FICO score.

So why is debt so significant to a score? For that matter, how can debt be such a burden to cause such a strain and turmoil on relationships? The short answer, it controls everything. Most importantly in relationships, it manages "time and money" I'll explain that later. For now, and an even shorter answer, stress.

As an underwriter, one of the first things I looked at on an application and credit report is the debt-to-income ratio and the debt-to-credit ratio.

The first, debt-to-income ratio, would tell me the financial stress of the potential borrower. A rule of thumb for me is to stay below 40% in fact 40% was a little on the high side depending on what type of product I was underwriting.

Think of when you applied for anything, credit card, car, etc. and you list your income. What people typically list is their gross income (before taxes and deduction). The credit report will show your credit cards, car payments, mortgage, student loans, etc. What is not shown is your cell phone, utilities, rent, insurance, etc. So already the underwriter is not working with entirely accurate information. For this reason, as an underwriter, I wanted to make sure there was enough room for variables and misstated information.

The second ratio is the debt-to-credit ratio, often referred to as "utilization." This number is another financial stress indicator or potential stress. For example, if you have a credit card with a credit line of $1,000, and you typically revolve a balance of $500 and pay the minimum payment. If this is your only card; this means your debt to credit ratio is 50%. This is high; this says that half of your credit available is used which can be an indication of higher risk. As an underwriter, I would look at around 30%.

Now I will say that in my time as an underwriter, things happen and a lot of times I would never rely on merely credit reports and numbers to make a decision. That is something that we will get into also in a later chapter. A lot of times I would talk to the borrower and to determine the reason of what was on the credit report that indicated risk or stress that would help with my decision. The point is debt can take a lot of if not most of our income, time to make income, and ultimately create stress if it is not controlled.

In speaking with one of the members of my site, she indicated that she and her ex never discussed credit until it was too late. When she learned of his credit issues which were debt, it was after she'd married the gentleman. The problem is that he had a gambling addiction and he accumulated the debt from this. Naturally, this caused strain on their marriage and her finances which led to a divorce for the couple and bankruptcy for her.

That member is just one of many stories I've heard over the years, I've heard some even worse. For example, the debt of a member's now ex-spouse accumulated because of drug and alcohol addictions. The problem was masked due to the ex's credit being exhausted so he was limited to what she, his wife could access, this him a functioning addict. When they married this, he gained not only trust but access to credit. It wasn't long before he binged and their marriage and lives were utterly destroyed.

Outside of these and other worst-case scenarios, debt is commonly accumulated, and even under the best case scenario, it can be stressful. When you marry someone or also if you are in a serious relationship with someone you take on their debt. I'm not saying you it belongs to you legally or your credit reports merge, in fact, that it is one of the biggest misconceptions of credit and relationships. However, when you plan a life with someone, and you begin a family. Naturally, you share expenses and budget together. If I have $100,000 in debt and the future Mrs. Green has $100,000 in debt, we collectively have $200,000 in debt. It doesn't matter whose name it's in or how it's divided. I wouldn't want to be a part of the conversation telling a future wife "No I only have $20,000 in debt, you have $180,000 in debt,

I don't know what you are going to do, but I'm going to pay my $20,000 off and buy a sports car." I'm sure I would be single for a long time with that type of thinking.

The goal is to have a realistic and honest conversation about; I call it "ghost of credit past, present, and future." Talk about what debt you have from the past, i.e., student loans, past relationships, etc. Talk about where you are currently, what are your current credit obligations, how many active credit cards do you have? How do you use them? How do you pay them? What is your car payment and mortgage payment? Finally, what are your plans, goals, and expectations for the future, what is your plans to pay those credit cards off? How about the loans and mortgage? He or she may be able to understand now that you are serious about them but this is why you are always insisting that you both pay for yourselves on your dates. You can stop making excuses for the getting out of dates or having a date without spending money. Again, I'm joking, but seriously, if your serious about the person you are dating, work together, if one is lacking, make sure they are educated by the stronger.

That is a little ahead of ourselves before we get to the plan of overcoming the problem that we've determined, let us define it. In the introduction, I indicated that you would be underwriters. Underwriters use tools to analyze the borrower. Most of our tools are observations and questions.

I go back to my Aunt Michelle and her teachings. This is a great tool, self-evaluation. Evaluate what you can or willing to handle and take on. This is not exclusively for finance, but also, in the relationship emotionally, mentally, romantically, etc. Apply real-world scenarios to what you are currently involved.

If you've experienced them already, use this as a litmus test to help. Look at you "Debt-to-Income" and "Debt-to-Credit" ratios, figuratively and literally. Can you take on more financial, emotional, or mental debt? How do you change in response to stress, good or bad?

I know I have dated women who transformed into different women under stress and pressure. I think of this visually as a scene for the movie, "I'm Gonna Get You Sucka." In the scene, the leading actress was being pursued by two guys who wanted to harm her. In the film she had "cramps" it was her "time of the month," and she turned into a literal monster.

While this was hilarious, I'm not saying women turn into creatures during their cycle. In fact, this depiction has nothing to do with a cycle, and it is not to sound misogynistic. I merely want to make the point that stress can cause a man or woman to turn into something completely different than what we know.

Conversely, sometimes stress can cause people to rise to the occasion and show a confident and more attractive side of them. Sometimes we won't see that until they are in a situation that demands this transformation. I believe this is part of our "fight or flight" response. The medical name for this is "Acute Stress Response," as Walter Cannon, a scientist, neurologist, and physiologist, described in his 1915 theory, "Bodily Changes in Pain, Hunger, Fear, and Rage: An Account of Recent Researches into the function of Emotional Excitement."

Primarily, when we experience stressful events, our bodies and minds react in 1 of 2 ways; either resist the event, or fight, or breakdown, or runaway, flight. Sometimes flight, causes people to have medical symptoms and cause illness mentally or physically. There is a lot of medical research and information on this topic; again I'm not a doctor, I can't delve into deep. I just want to provide context to explain why we do some of the things we do. As well as, why maybe we should or shouldn't do things.

With this being said, evaluate what type of person you are, fight or flight. Are you a fighter, in financially stressful situations while others take flight? Evaluate your partner or future partner. As I mentioned earlier, debt can cause stress, even indirectly. This is why it's important to have these discussions early on in the relationship.

Out of the millions of dollars in tools and software that the banks used that I worked for, the best tool I used that was the most effective was the great conversation.

"Talking about money is still Taboo in our communities, I don't know why. What a person earns is a private matter. However, we should dispel that farce as well, because if you want to be with me, we have to share money, if we have to pay these bills especially if we're going to have kids. We can't keep secrets about how much we make and how much we spend." - Kier

CHAPTER 4 - BUT WHAT'S CREDIT GOT TO DO WITH IT?

"Everything" - Sean Johnson, General Manager, Porsche Delaware

Being in the car sales industry for decades, Sean has seen many situations. He explains how patterns he's observed in normal business are relatable to relationships.

"There was a customer who we noticed a pattern that indicated some financial stress. The customer would have his car serviced on days that would allow him to use the service car for trips and weekends. He would even delay having the car serviced to ensure he would have more time to use the service car. - Sean Johnson

As Sean noticed the pattern, he thought, "His relationship won't last long." Speaking regarding the customer's significant other who also became a customer. The woman had a great career and credit to match. Her boyfriend, the questionable customer, attempted to advise her on the best decisions to make. This advice would be ideal if the gentleman were a credible source. His credit score was substantially lower.

The couple eventually would separate over credit and finance differences, proving Sean correct.

"We see it in this business all the time. He messed my credit up, or she ruined my credit. Partners and spouses were taking on cars they can't afford or trying to get out of cars they shouldn't have had." - Sean Johnson

Our credit histories impact many facets of our lives today, credit cards and loans to employment and insurance. But why, why is it that the $53 cable bill that you could have paid three years ago, however, you were "making a point" is now causing you to have higher insurance, interest rates, and denials? Short answer, Risk.

So, what does credit have to do with relationships? What can what you know about someone's credit history tell you about them? Short answer, risk. Short of apparent personal information, a lot. In fact, over the years as a credit underwriter, boyfriend, and as a consumer, I have learned and continue to discover the many correlations between credit histories and interpersonal relationships.

Let's start at the surface level, the actual score. In the last chapter, I mentioned that the Fair Isaac Company calculates a score for you, FICO score from credit data. Other companies such as Experian, Transunion, and Equifax also do the same. These corporations are who we in the United States use for our credit reports, and they have their scoring systems too, however, for the sake of this example we'll use the score that most lenders use, FICO. They have provided the breakdown which is also available on their website. However, here is their calculation breakdown:

35% Payment History

30% Amounts Owed

15% Length of Credit History

10% New Credit

10% Credit Mix

This breakdown tells us how we pay based on history, late or on time. How much debt we currently carry. How long we've had credit or how much experience we have. What type of credit we have, i.e., Mortgage, Credit cards, Student or Auto loans, etc.

From this are we balanced, experienced, or stressed? Do we honor our commitments? Again, as an underwriter in simplest terms, my job was to determine the relationship between the borrower and the bank. The score and report helped me to assess the likelihood of default.

From this information provided in the report let's say there was a pattern of late payments that started one month after the accounts opened. Those same accounts would then default after the 6th month. It is likely that borrower would continue this pattern with us upon approval. Especially if there are no other accounts that were satisfied. If we were to examine deeper we could investigate this for fraud. However, we could save that for a different conversation. We will summarize this application decision as denial and agree does not honor commitments.

How would we relate this to dating? Aside from evidence of bad credit history, this person has a pattern of starting financial commitments with no intention of finishing. Some could argue what if something happened? True, they did make a payment or two. They opened other accounts and attempted to open others without satisfying defaulted accounts.

Now apply this scenario to a relationship, this is a habit that some couples learn in relationships at the wrong times, often when it is too late. For example, you meet this same borrower and are amazed by their charm, personality, and physically attracted to them. Months maybe even years go by, and your relationship has reached an earnest level. If you are not married, you both are either considering it or planning for it. One day they ask you to apply for this excellent offer for something they want. You want to love them so naturally, you want them to be happy. They've assured you they'll take care of the payment.

You've agreed, this is the first of several accounts that have been opened. Six months later, it is time to get a new home for any possible reason. That is when it happens, at the mortgage brokers office you receive the shock of your life. Your perfect credit history was just denied your dream home. Your better half is not there with you, conveniently, they had an emergency at work.

I would love to say this was a figment of my imagination. However, I had a borrower that this happened. They didn't check their credit history often, only when they made significant purchases because they paid everything on-time. They applied for the card for their significant other and thought no more about it because it was for them and they were to pay for it, never to hear about it again until they met with the mortgage company. By then it was already in default, and there were several accounts.

Conversely, with a conversation at the beginning of the relationship, they could have learned about their payment habits and potential "risk" of the person that ruined their credit and dream of owning a home at the time.

This is just one example and thing that credit can tell us about people and relationships. We can delve deeper and talk about the patterns as it relates to trust. Aside from things that may happen in life and I'm not immune to them, medical issues, natural disasters, layoffs, divorces, etc. Many things can affect a person's credit history. However, the conversation should be the determining factor of the correlation between the person and their history.

When we talk about credit histories and its ability to show trust or lack thereof, it's those who merely intentionally don't pay or honor their commitments. Just like those who don't acknowledge their relationship commitments deliberately, as in infidelity.

While this is not an exact science but it has been my experience that as creatures of habits if a person is not willing to honor their financial commitments, why would they commit to an interpersonal relationship? Again, not speaking of a person who has had challenges that caused credit issues. This person's other qualities typically will shine, and you'll be able to determine in further conversation. This is valuable information that is worth the discussion to learn the potential mates spending and repayment habits. These things can offer insight into how they value and honor commitment.

My associate and I were talking in my office, and we joked, "if they won't commit to keeping their phone on, why would they commit to a relationship. People are building their lives with pre-paid people with post-pay expectations." That may be a little facetious, yet, the point is solid and precise. How can you expect someone who doesn't take something as serious as their finances or financial obligations to regard your relationship seriously?

Another item I looked at in correlation of credit history and interpersonal relationships was debt. Now I will admit I'm going out there with this one but bear with me it'll make sense. I mentioned the "Debt-to-Credit" percentage or "Utilization" previously. The formula is total balance divided by total credit available (i.e. Credit available $10,000, balances $2,500, 2500/10000=.25 or 25% utilization). This says the borrower has good moderation of their credit spending of what's available to them. Keywords in the last statement, MODERATION, AVAILABLE TO THEM.

Applying this to the dating world and reversing the ratio to say 75% utilization would say there may be an issue of moderation. Not to objectify anyone but let us equate credit card accounts to relationships for a moment for the sake of example. The total balance of the accounts is still $10,000, but it's broken up into ten accounts or 10 relationships or 10 people you are seeing. You are 75% utilized, which means that your total balance in all accounts or relationships is $7,500.

Remember in my explanation of "Debt to Credit" in the previous chapter that as an underwriter, I viewed this as potential stress. Let's take away the financial aspect of the ten accounts and equate the utilization to the normal relationship or dating requirement, i.e., time; phone calls walks, dates, gifts, etc. This assumption means that you are 25% away from being completely maxed out of your ability "dating", in this example. If you are dating ten people at one time "God bless you", I'm sure you can attest that this is taxing on you mentally, emotionally, and financially. Back to the financial example with 75% utilization, you would only be $2,500 away from being maxed out of all of your credit lines. This indicates entirely to much potential stress which makes for potential risk, which without discussion and sufficient explanation leads to denial.

I told you I was going out there, but the point is one of the things that credit displays to us, moderation levels. In other words, how well the person moderates and how much willpower they may have, if we want to get more in-depth. However, let us just look at moderation. Merriam - Webster defines moderation as "An avoidance of extremes in one's actions, beliefs, or habits." Lack of restraint is what seems to get people in trouble.

Having a drink in moderation is not what causes problems. Maxing out your credit cards for special occasions, holidays, vacations, etc. with a plan to pay the balances off does not mean you have spending or credit problems. Living on credit cards, buying things well above your means, and maxing out credit cards with no record of why does, however, indicate a problem.

The key is moderation, and I'm no different, I had to learn about moderation as it relates to several things in life. I believe there is a saying "Things are best served in moderation." It holds true because there are no after effects to whatever you receive or do. Be it food, alcohol, or spending; you don't face horrible sometimes life-altering repercussions when things are in moderation.

Dating is no different, how can you honestly have the chance to know if the person you are dating is the one for you if you are spread out over 10? How can you pay down ten cards from 75% if you are payments are spread out over 10? Of course, there is a way, but it will be taxing and stressful.

In the purest form, it comes down to trust and finance. The word finance is not by any means to be mistaken for money, however, the ability to manage money or said finance. Merriam-Webster defines finance as "money or other liquid resources of a government, business, group, or individual." While defining credit as "a record of how well you have paid your bills in the past." Credit, as it relates to relationships, can tell us about our potential mates and life partners.

CHAPTER 5 - SERIOUSLY, RELATIONSHIPS, RELATIONSHIPS, SERIOUSLY?

It feels like long gone are the days or so it seems when relationships were long lasting, built on trust, and security. The foundations of our households were established on the sanctity and union of the serious relationships that started them. For example, I can remember my grandparents. It seemed to be a pretty simple formula; he'd work she'd make the home and manage the finances.

Though at the time I didn't think too much of it, there was a lot of trust in what seemed so simple and every day. What I mean is, she trusted him to leave home, work, and return with income. Enough to provide and sustain their lifestyle. He trusted her to care for the family, make the home, and manage his hard earned income without question. My grandmother worked early on in their relationship, and collectively they decided for her to be a full-time homemaker.

There must've been something to their system; their union lasted 55 years, bore four beautiful children, six grandchildren, with all of their children going to college.

As I got older and began to experience life for myself, I began to experience some of the differences and similarities in their relationships and others, primarily working in the banks. I learned how financially savvy my grandmother was and why she handled the finances.

To this day, no one will confirm or deny, but I'm pretty sure my grandmother was a day trader. I'm talking about before the "ETrades, Scottrades" and other online brokerages. She taught me about investing and the stock market.

This was my first indication that maybe I had some of these perceptions wrong about money, who made it, how it is made, and finally the term "homemaker."

Aside from the finance component of their relationship, although it's a massive component in every relationship, every other element smoothly flowed that I can remember. Granted, I was young, but I'm pretty sure I would remember if not scared if there were memories of my grandparents fighting or yelling. Fortunately, that was never the case.

I equate this to the large component of finance being handled and addressed well before I was the twinkle in my mother's eye. Assuming finance makes up 75% of relationships, 25% the rest, whatever that may be. If you address the 75% of what could go wrong in your relationship look at all the time and energy you have to focus on the "whatever." Yes, let your minds and imaginations wander. Making your thoughts and fantasies wonder in a relationship strengthens it.

How great would it be to explore and learn new things with your partner and best friend? For instance, traveling exploring new places because, hey, the budget allows it and it's what you both love to do and what you have in common. How about instead of fighting over bills or spending ours not talking and finding ways not to be in the same room or house, you spend hours making love with your significant other because they are the most beautiful person in the world to you. You're not stressed because your bills are under control because you both worked out a plan and system. You never notice how beautiful he or she looks in this shade of "stress-free."

These are just some examples, but it's entirely up to you, the point is, your relationship is astonishing with the burden of stress lifted off of the both of you, and that is why relationships are long-lasting.

"We have to dispute those beliefs of what we think finance regarding marriage is and what it isn't. We have to have assigned roles, sometimes it's the man that's the financial planner, and the woman is the provider, but this is a new era, and everybody has to work. However, the point is to be humble and share your weakness and say maybe I'm not good at math. An example of my wife and I, my wife is a control freak; she controls the finances. I get no shut-off notices, always food in the fridge, if I want a toy, I tell her, she tells me when. So she's that person, me I provide I have the business, multiple streams of income I tell her, Girl just take this check." - Kier Berkel

CHAPTER 6 - THE C'S OF ~~CREDIT~~, LOVE

So you're there the point where you met that person who may be worth your time, love, affection, admiration, etc. What do you look for? Granted, I know we all may have our specific tastes, likes, dislikes, etc. Let's delve deeper and talk about the foundation. Consider this, if they weren't attractive or they couldn't dress, they wouldn't have received your attention, right? If they didn't have a personality that kept your attention or stimulated your mind, they wouldn't even be in the running to be your man or woman, correct? So we don't need to discuss that.

What we do need to discuss however is the proper tools and l things to look for to make the "approval" if you will. If you remember from earlier in the book, I stated I would teach you to be "Love Underwriters." I also mentioned that the best tool is communication.

The thing about communication is that you need to know two fundamental things, what message do you hope to receive or identify, and what message do you use to receive that message honestly and accurately. Meaning, how do I get them to tell me what it is I need to know without directly asking them in some cases. This information can prevent setting them up to deceive you even it wasn't intentional. It also stops them from feeling uncomfortable and you as well.

85

For instance, you would just come right out and ask, "How many people have you slept with?" while comparing your favorite wines. I mean I know people who have and do, maybe it works for them but for most people it doesn't.

So let's start with what information we hope to obtain in this line of communication. Going back to the world of credit underwriting, remember earlier in the book I mention credit underwriting or analysis is the first step of collections. With that principle, we approach the application knowing what we don't want. We don't want borrowers who don't honor their commitments. We don't want borrowers who can't repay their loans or financial obligations to us. We are cautious with borrowers who are not stable.

This view is from a lending standpoint, however, look at its application to relationship environment. Would you want a mate that doesn't have a history of honoring their commitments? Would you want a mate that doesn't have the ability (maturity, mentality, health, etc.) to honor their commitment to you? Finally, would you want a mate that is not stable, without acceptable reason? The answer would be no. Remember again, without judgment their may be a reason for a specific answer. This is the reason why communication is essential, to fully understand what the answers are and why they may be.

We simplify this line of questioning with the acronym S.A.W.:

• **Stability** – Are they stable; do they know what they want out of life, are they working? What's their living situation? Do they have their own home or residence?

• **Ability** – Do they have the ability to commit or be in a relationship with you? Are they mature enough to be in the type of relationship you want? Do they have the mentality that is on your level? Do they think like you or how you feel you mate should think? Are they financial compatible with you? Not necessarily if they have a similar income as yours or not, but does their financial goals and management match yours? Are they mentally or emotionally attached to someone else or a past relationship? Are they still in a relationship?

- Willingness – Are they willing to commit or be in the same type of relationship you are looking for? What are their intentions with you? What are they looking for? Why aren't they in a relationship? Have they been in a relationship before? What happened in the previous relationship?

These questions are adaptive to your relationship goals and ideals in a partner as long as they allow you to accurately assess the foundation or the S.A.W. of your potential mate. I wish I could tell you what answers are acceptable but just as in lending from product to product and bank to bank, the criteria for approval is different. It comes down to what works for you and what you are willing to accept.

A few things I want to remind you is to communicate, have conversations. Believe it or not, banks are not in business to deny applicants, although if you're on the receiving end of a denial, it can certainly feel that way. In that same manner, you shouldn't set your mind to find a reason, not to date or go to another level with this particular person. This is just a guide to cautiously move forward, to precisely know what it is you are getting involved with and manage your relationship accordingly.

Conversely, don't go into the situation to optimistic, ignoring red flags. The saying is "What happens in the wash eventually comes out in the rinse." This no different, you can ignore flags like no consistent job history or never been in a relationship longer than one month. However, once you find out the reason for those things, it will most certainly affect your relationship. Even in more relevant circumstances, credit, you don't want to be in the situation like the mortgage borrower.

Imagine yourself learning about the red flag that you ignored at the worst possible time. We can see how conditions like that can cause a significant strain on relationships. Alternatively, we notice how having conversations, understanding, and accurately knowing your mate can alleviate stress in relationships.

Remember from our discussion about stress and "fight or flight," the importance of knowing or at least having an idea of how our future responds to stress? It is also essential, to be honest with yourself about how you react to stress. If not, one of these scenarios could lead to a very stressful situation. These ultimately cause, in most cases relationship ending problems. We can see how conditions like that can cause a significant strain on relationships. Furthermore, why finance is the leading cause of divorce.

Industry-wide in lending, underwriters look at something called the "Three C's of Credit" to assess applicants. The Three C's", similar to "S.A.W." tells us foundational things about our applicants. In the case of this book, it tells us the foundational things about our potential mates.

The "Three C's" are:

• **Character or Credit History** – Tells us how a borrower managed their credit in the past and present to give us an idea of what they will do in the future. What kind of accounts do they have currently or have they had? What is their payment history currently and previously? How often are they requesting a new credit account? Do they have a lot of inquiries? What type of inquiries do they have? Are they employed? If so, how long? If not, why not? What is their residence scenario? Do they rent, own, or live with relatives? How long have they lived there?

• **Capacity** – What is their income? What is their debt to income ratio? Do they have disposable income? Are they self-employed or employed (this tells the frequency of income, self-employed may not receive income depending on what happens with business while employed may be more dependable) What are their monthly expenses that may not be reported on the credit report? What are the terms and amount of what they are applying for? (For example, if it's a mortgage, how long is the term, 15,30, etc.? How much is the payment? If credit card, what is the max line?) How do the products affect the applicant's financial picture (Will the mortgage payment increase the debt to income ratio above 40%?)

• **Collateral or Capital** – How much does the applicant have in savings, retirement, investments, etc.? It applying for secured loan or product, how much is applicant using as a down payment? (I.e., Applicant is making a $5,000 down payment on a new car.) If application is for a mortgage product, what is the property used for (i.e., Primary home, second, investment, etc.) How much equity is on the property? What is the Loan-to-Value? (How much is owed or will be owed vs. how much the home or property is worth?) What is the purpose of the product or loan? (Is it a cash-out refinance or a rate and term refinance? In other words, is the applicant looking to use the equity in the home or just lower the rate, payment, or change the term of the loan?)

You can see, it more detailed with most of the answers coming from the application and credit report, yet, this still has the same purpose as S.A.W. Are they stable, are they able, and do they have the willingness to pay or repay? Applying "The Three C's" to love, we would look in conversation to understand the character of the person we're considering to be our mate. We would also look at their capacity, are they able to fit us in their lives and share our goals? What is their collateral? In do they have to support what they are saying?

For instance, you meet someone who says they want to be a doctor or lawyer, what are they doing to show that is true or they're sincere? Are they in school? Are they complaining about student loans? Have they taken any number of exams or in an intern or residency programs?

How about they love your business acumen, and they blurt out, "Well I have my own business?" What do they have to show that is true besides the same day printed business card that "accidentally" fell out of their pocket? Ask them about said aspiration or goals, someone with ambition or goal that consumes that much of their life usually will talk in great detail about it to just about anyone who will listen. This is especially true for someone they are trying to impress.

I know starting any one of my businesses, I waited for the moment that someone would give me any indicator to talk about business. This isn't vanity in most cases or bragging. We are proud and passionate about what we are doing. With that being said, people who are that involved with an aspiration or goal should be experts, or so it would sound to us unless, of course, we also are in the same industry or line of work. In either case, listen for inconsistencies in their explanation and stories.

When in doubt ask for proof. As an underwriter, especially with credit cards, we would often have people whose credit report did not match what they were saying or their application. We would at that point request proof of anything for income to assets. "Ok Mr. John Doe, you make $2,000,000 per year with $10,000,000 in the bank?" Meanwhile, Mr. Doe's credit report shows maxed out $500 credit cards with scattered late payments on a mortgage for $600 per month. While his application shows, he owns his home outright with no payment.

While this is an extreme example, you can see why we would want to verify his income. I can say I had a similar situation when an applicant had low credit lines and mortgage payments that didn't match what he was saying or his application. I requested the proof, which was correct and valid. It turned out; the gentleman never used credit. The credit on his file was all for his son. He placed everything in his name for his son, and his son just couldn't handle the responsibility, which is more than likely why the man had everything in his name for his son because his son's credit was ruined.

The point, I would have never known if, A. I didn't ask about it, B. I didn't request the proof, and C. Most importantly, I didn't know the flags to look for that indicated something was wrong.

CHAPTER 7 - DATING IN A RISKY WORLD

In a New York Times article that we were mentioned in on Christmas 2012, there was a line that read "Credit Scores are like the dating equivalent of a sexually transmitted disease test." That's sound a little extreme, however, when you think of what we go through in this world on a day to day basis, even as individuals, we would like to A. be protected, and B. know who we are trusting with our lives and finances.

In relationships, we face a lot of challenges external and internally. In most cases, the internal problems are caused by the outer and the past. What is the most significant culprit of these challenges? You guessed it, finances. It could be financed challenges of the past it could be something that's entirely out of either one of you control but affects you both financially, but it causes strain on the relationship. A lot of times these relationships don't recover.

Think of a breakup, could be your own or someone you know. Now I pose these two questions, 1. Was the breakup over finances? Even if he or she cheated, think about the first argument or when you or the person this applies to first started to notice or feel discontentment in the relationship. Did something financial happen or change? Loss of job, unexpected bill, tragedy, large purchase, natural disaster, etc. Now that this is established, 2. Did you or the person this applies to say, "Man, they changed, I've never seen he or she like this before. They're a completely different person. etc." Remember, "fight or flight," or acute stress response.

Let me say first; I'm sorry if I brought up painful memories. I promise this was not my intention. I wanted you to see how finances can affect relationships. Wait, it not just finances, on to the second question. It's not that the person has changed, that person was there. You never saw how that person responded under that type of pressure.

This is the same whether you were the cause of the financial issue or not. Think about the last chapter where we assessed the person's "Three C's" or "S.A.W." Within the either "Character" or even the "Ability" assessment, you could determine what type of person he or she is if things were to get bad. It all goes back to what happened with past relationships and are they mature and can their mentality handle a "serious relationship."

Those are surface level questions and evaluations; deeper would pertain to finances. Were you and this person financially compatible? Did you share the same financial goals? Did you determine who was stronger financially? By this, I don't mean who made the most money, but who handle finances the best? By discovering these things early on, you would be able to see how this person is under financially stressful conditions or if they would put you in a financially stressful situation.

Remember in the last chapter; I talked about "Collateral" in relationships? When in doubt, ask for proof. I'm not saying ask them for their proof of income or assets, but at the point that you and this person are dating seriously or considering it, have "what if" conversations and simulations. Call it "financial, real-world role-playing" and add some excitement to your relationship. Yes, I am a little facetious, but in all seriousness have conversations about these matters and discuss what roles and actions you would take in such events. For instance, use past situations if you've experienced them or if you haven't, use something from history. These could be anything from a job loss or loss of hours to a natural disaster. This exercise is also useful for planning good things even not just adverse scenarios.

Say for example you meet someone and you both determine that you want to have the Tudor style home with the white picket fence, matching Volvos, and 2.3 kids. I know it's not possible to have a third of a child, but I'm always reminded of those studies where they said: "The average American household has 2.3 kids." Back to our example and your Tudor style home and perfect life. Because you have these things in common and you both get excited about it, why not plan it out.

Determine what it would take to reach that goal. Plan what roles each of you would choose to achieve it. Have fun with it, make a date night of it and create cute vision boards.

Doing this will help bring you two closer together and have your plan and dreams in-sync. This exercise is part of "acting your dreams out with open eyes" together. Even in the conversations and simulations with adverse scenarios, you two will be brought closer together, and you will prepare each other for such events, should they arise.

These exercises have no right or wrong answers or solutions. They merely exercise to determine opportunities to improve upon and to assess who's more equipped to handle what. For example, you may be the one who is better at money management. You may have already known this, but now your partner sees this in a real-world setting and why it's essential. Your partner may be more inspirational or motivational. They may be the voice you need in a situation to keep you calm and focused on the goal or surviving whatever negative situation may have arisen. Either way, by these strengths and weakness being exposed proactively. This route is much better than learning about this in the middle of a crisis or after you both impulsively decide to buy the Tudor style home or the 2 Volvos while living in their parent's basement.

This opportunity is a great time to talk about something I'm asked about in different countries, languages, settings, media formats, etc. by friends, family, journalists, and even celebrities. Credit scores, when to talk about them. There is no definitive answer to this question. It honestly depends on you, your relationship goals, and the person you're dating or considering dating.

For the record, I wouldn't say ask someone their credit score randomly in the middle of the nightclub after three drinks and dancing to Drake's "Hotline Bling."

Why, naturally because it's not a proper setting for a serious conversation. Not that "Hotline Bling" is not a great song to get telephone numbers too. People may say but your dating site matches people based on that, and they're mostly exchanging their credit scores before knowing each other. Well, not entirely, the difference is my members come to my site looking for serious relationships, and they want to match with a single person with the same financial mindset as them.

So when is a good time to discuss it? I would say when you feel comfortable that this is someone you think you'd consider having a serious relationship with. It could be "love at first sight" it could be ten dates. It honestly depends on you and your chemistry with that person and how they align with your relationship and life goals. Nonetheless, this discussion is vital in determining not only is this person financially compatible with you but are they compatible with you overall.

This person may make a million dollars per year but have horrible credit. It's up to you to determine why that is the case. Maybe they are too busy to pay their bills on time. Maybe they just have all around horrible money management skills. Perhaps their credit suffered a significant hit from a divorce, business loss, catastrophe. Most importantly, if this person is worth it, maybe you can help with your superior money management skills. The thing of the yin-yang sign and the saying "opposites attract," you may not make as much as this person, but you have perfect credit. Think of what kind of power couple you could be, filling each other's voids. Listen to me, I just played matchmaker with you and an imaginary person, damn, I'm good.

Pardon me for my moment of vanity, just wanted to make sure you are still with me. Even if a person doesn't have the best credit in the world per se, it can tell you a lot. Not just negative things, what if it told you positive things? What if someone with a marginal, average, or below average score told you things that possibly make the deal? No, I'm not crazy, and this is not one of my sarcastic joking moments. First, it would depend on you, what you are looking for, and your relationship goals. Second, you would have to converse and delve into why the person's score is in this range.

My older cousin used to say to me, "I'd go to war with a soldier in a tattered uniform before a soldier in a new uniform any day." He told me this years ago, as I prepared to write this book, I thought about it. That saying means that the soldier in the tattered uniform has gone to war and returned. The soldier is war-tested, has been in battle and returned to tell about it, knowing what to expect and most importantly how to survive.

Let's apply this to dating, sure a person with perfect credit may look amazing, but it also says that they may not have experienced some of the hardships that may come. Now, I'm not saying that anyone with perfect credit has never had anything bad happen to them. Furthermore, I do not wish anything unfortunate happen to anyone. If I had it my way, this would be a perfect world where we never experienced any hardships. Unfortunately, that's not the world we live in. There are some people with excellent credit or ideal credit that have experienced worse things than we could imagine but they recovered, and they remained consistent since that recovery. Remember, most thing stay on your credit file for seven years, some ten depending what it is.

People ask me about credit all of the time, and another misconception is about the length items stay on the credit report. Someone will say to me, "Niem, I've had this account on my credit report that's hurting my credit." I'll naturally ask about the item. The common response is similar to this, "Well, it's an account I haven't had in years, at least 7." To which I'd inquire if it was paid and when. This question is where the misconception comes into play. "Well, no but it's seven years old, so it should be removed, correct?" Unfortunately, that is not correct; it is seven years from the last date the company reported, at which point the credit reporting agency should remove it. If the bill was never paid and the creditor reports every month for seven years as not paid, it will continue to report this information. This would be the same if they sold it to a collection agency. If there is a genuine inaccuracy, you should take steps to dispute the error.

Getting back to the point, take a moment and think about in your lifetime what disasters you may have experienced or could have experienced. Once again I'm not trying to dredge up painful memories, simply making a point. If you weren't of age to be affected financially or in a region that would have affected you, imagine for a moment if you were. How many times would that have been in your lifetime? Exclude health issues, just think of natural disasters, terrorist attacks, recession, etc. In my life, there has been 9/11 and the economic meltdown of 2008. 9/11 affected my first job. Those are just two that I'll disclose for the benefit of this example. Those two were huge; they hit economies all over the world. If I were to name all the things that went or can go wrong, this would be the guide to disasters. I'm sure we can agree that unfortunately, we live in a world where things go wrong that affect us all.

When someone has a score that is marginal or average, they have been through something. It reflects that they have experienced financial stress caused by personal issue, i.e., job loss, health, etc. or external issues natural disasters, economic disasters, acts of terror, etc. How can this be a dealmaker? Well, it would depend on the conversation. First question, why is the score so low? What are your plans to correct it? Depending on the answer to these questions and the other factors that you are considering about this person, this should be a dealmaker or breaker.

Remember in my example a little while back about the application not coinciding with the credit report? This is similar, does this person show signs of recovery? Did they tell you they have a 500 credit score, but they seem to make a decision that reflects poor money management? For instance, they live with their parents to recover from whatever financial catastrophe, i.e., divorce, job loss, etc. You notice they're either at the club every weekend spending money like they're a celebrity. Are they more focused on getting a new car than moving out of their parent's basement? Is he or she king or queen Midas payday weekend then the next week they're on a mysterious diet because they can't afford to eat? Chances are they haven't learned their lesson, and they should be a relationship denial.

However, if they never go out and they are saving money everywhere they can decide to build a business so they'll never be put in the situation of losing their job again and have to monitor their credit score like people watch football scores, it is safe to say, they've learned their lesson.

You may say, "That's good, they've learned their lesson, but what does that mean for me?" Remember my cousin's saying, well this soldier has returned from war. When things happen that we hope won't but prepare if they do, this person has been through it. They are a resource of everything from the feelings of how to deal with changes that may occur to the steps of recovery. They are also now conditioned on what to reinforce what you already practice, this time with a vengeance.

Think about a fire, if you've never been burned by it, yet, you never dared touch it why? Because someone told you not to and the consequences of your actions. I can assure you the reason we know and are told not to touch it is because someone somewhere played with it and got burned. They began to say to people or people who witnessed said, "Hey man, you might not want to touch that, Johnny did and it tore him up."

It is one thing to hear something that is bad and can happen, but it's completely different to hear it and have it reinforced by someone who witnessed or experienced it.

Conversely, your good habits can rub off on them. You can reinforce the benefits of having good credit and money management skills. This would see their potential goal in real time.

The goal is to be prepared for what may come at you, your mate, and your relationship in this dangerous world of unexpected circumstances. Our relationships should enhance us, make us stronger, smarter, etc. This is why it is vital that we are selective when it comes to choosing who we want to be with. This is because they are us and we are them. They may have to fight with you again odds, adversity, tragedy, and external forces that may come your way.

I've always been taught that your home is your safe zone. You fight all day to conquer goals, act out dreams, prove yourself in a world that seemingly may be against you. But home is where you rest and recover. How can you survive if you have to fight in the world and your home? How can a relationship survive if someone is fighting or seemingly fighting against you? You can't, and this is why most relationships are doomed because people try to carry too much on their shoulders in a relationship. No matter the intention, whether it is pride or love, whether it's genuine or just to say they did it. Relationships are 50/50, not 60/40, 80/20, 90/10, or anything less than even. Finances in a relationship are no different. I can't stress this enough, this is not about asset value or income but how it's handled. It doesn't matter how the $100,000 comes in the house, what makes the difference is how it goes out. The money management is what's important and what helps or hurts it, whether it's past present or future. The key is communication about the past, present, and future.

CHAPTER 8 - LOVE, LIFE, AND FINANCE: IT'S ALL A ROLLERCOASTER RIDE, BUCKLE UP!

People close to me would tell you I never have a day that is all bad or all good. My days much like life, love, and finances are like a rollercoaster. Ups and downs, twists and turns dips and dives. This doesn't bother me; I'm used to it, more importantly, I'm prepared.

But how do you prepare for a day that can be one extreme to the next? Well to answer this question, I resort back to the wisdom of my cousin. He said, "Nye, you have to be even keel." He said to keep a calm disposition with everything no matter how good or bad. There are days when I would receive multimillion-dollar offers and days when I would lose tons of money. There are days when I'm doing press around the world, and then there are days when meetings, speaking engagements, and other significant events get canceled last minute. I used to be a live wire, and if you were around me, you would hear it. This was no way to live or have others living around me.

The point I wish to make in this personal example is that sometimes the best preparation is to adjust our expectations. But to change your expectations, you have first to know what you expect. Furthermore, if these expectations involve another person they must know what you expect of them and vice versa.

I hear things all the time from random people about how so and so let them down. But so and so didn't know what was expected of them. Thus how could they possibly prevent disappointment if they didn't know what was expected?

Would you date someone knowingly who would openly break an expectation or disappoint you? No, of course not. Going back to the credit report and what it tells us, remember it shows us how a person honors commitments. The banks and institutions, however, have to let the borrower know what the obligations and expectations they have of you honoring those responsibilities, correct? They do every chance they get from the application, to the statement, to the collection calls should it get to that point. Nonetheless, they let you know, or else they wouldn't be able to collect on the agreement, in fact, there would not be any. There would only be a bank giving you money.

My lawyer explained to me that an agreement or contract as a record of expectations. He said this is true no matter if it's the operating agreement between my corporation or an agreement between parties doing business together. This way the parties involved always know what's expected of them. The same is true with your card member agreement with your credit card provider. In fact, you reinforce that contract every time you sign the merchant copy of the receipt. The next time you make a purchase look at the little sentence generally below the signature line. It read something similar to this:

I agree to pay above total under the card issuer agreement.

So what does this have to do with relationships, dating, and love? Did I lose you yet? I hope not if so don't worry; I'm bringing back around right now. With all the ups and downs of love, life, and finances, shouldn't you know what to expect from your mate? Shouldn't they know what to expect from you? No, I'm not going to say have them sign a contract. Although, it's not too bad of an idea. It can be fun, a love contract, outlining the expectations of your relationship. Either way, the expectation should be explicitly discussed and described. However, be realistic and fair remember, "even keel." Remember relationships should be 50/50, don't place an expectation on someone that you couldn't live up to yourself.

Once your expectation has been set in place and outlined, you should communicate them to each other, remind each other. I'm not saying become like the bank leaving little notes around the house or making them sign for every action or gift of love and kindness with a line below that says:

I agree to fulfill my expectation according to the relationship agreement.

Don't send a statement and make collection calls either. Just make simple reminders, that even if they're needed. This protects the relationship between internal forces and challenges. When the core is solid and unified, the external forces are less efficacious against the relationship.

I sensed that you felt an example coming. Here it is, let's assume you have an expectation that your significant other tells you when they are approached by another person looking to date them. They do, and you know everything, in fact, you two have such great communication, that you joke about it. You then receive information about this person that approached your significant other. You are not shocked, in fact, you expected it because you and your mate already discussed it.

Conversely, let's say he or she never told you and you receive this same info. Do you begin to wonder why did your mate not tell you about this? Because the expectation wasn't fulfilled, there's room for external forces to bring problems and break down the relationship.

I took a different approach; nonetheless, you can see the importance of communication and expectations. When setting expectations, you must be mindful of for whom you're setting expectations. For instance, if you know your mate is not good with money, don't establish an expectation that has a reliance on money management. If you do, you are getting in the rollercoaster of love with no seatbelt. It's almost as if you're asking that person to disappoint you. Help your mate and guide them to understand as they grow your expectation of them should increase.

Remember the role-playing exercises we talked about previously? Setting expectations and creating the love contract can be a role-play exercise. The goal is to make you both stronger individually and as a couple while preparing your relationship for the ups and downs of life and love. This also allows you to get to know each other really, the things that make you happy and conversely your dislikes.

You both knew what it took to get together and start the relationship. You got passed the stage of favorite colors, wines, foods, etc. What about pet peeves, annoyances, stressors? Why find out at the point when they're annoying you, or you're irritating them? Why not find out proactively and learn to avoid it?

When you open a credit card, in your cardmember agreement, you learn that if you don't make your payment by your due date, there is a late fee. You know that if you send in a check that is not honored and returned there is a returned check fee. You know that once your payment is thirty days past due it is reported to the credit bureau and it affects your credit score. Why do you acknowledge this? Because these things are outlined in the expectations that are set in the card member agreement. Some of us are more familiar with what banks and companies expect from us than our mates and life partners. Does that seem right? Some of us apply the same principles of honoring commitments and expectations to all relationships and get along just fine. Some of us don't honor any obligations at all and wonder why we suffer in life and feel the entire world is against us.

In my first book, "Daydreaming Mogul's Guide Vol. 1: Daydreams and Success" I discussed "Luck." Not the mythical luck, such as charms and rabbits' feet. I explained that luck is when preparation meets opportunity. If you are prepared for opportunities to arise, you more than likely will have a positive outcome. With that being said, relationships take luck. The relationship needs preparation for not just the downs in love, life, and finance, but the ups as well.

Why should you be prepared for the "ups"? Well up signifies a change in direction. The key word is change, whether it is moving in together, marriage, addition to the family, additional income, lottery winnings, retirement, etc. Whatever it is or can be positive, it changes the normal life you may have experienced. Lack of preparation can turn even the most favorable situation into a negative circumstance.

Once again the easiest way to be prepared is to set reasonable "even-keeled" expectations. Set these expectations for yourself as well as your mate. This way you know "If this then that, if that then this." You will, and your mate will be lucky in love on the rollercoaster of love, life, and finance.

CHAPTER 9 - GOOD CREDIT IS SEXY!

On a radio interview some time back I did in Florida with David Holland. He asked me, "Is credit, good credit sexy?" Let's talk about this. Finally, we get to the main course of this book, the sexiness of credit. People often laugh and are puzzled when they hear my websites tagline "Where Good Credit is Sexy." This is because at first glance we don't look at credit as something sexy. We look at credit as something tedious. Numbers, bills, responsibilities, credit scores and reports. What could be sexy about that?

"You make good money, and your credit is good. You can get what you want when you want it. You're confident, and it shows in your stride. The same works for relationships, if both of you have good credit that's a major worry that's alleviated. Leaving more time to focus on what's important, the relationship and each other." - Sean Johnson, Porsche of Delaware

That's sexy, let's take away the scores and numbers and look at responsibilities. How do you view a person who takes control of their obligations? A man or woman who confidently moves through life taking care of their business without worry because they honor every commitment. In fact, they have the maturity not to take on responsibilities that they don't have the capacity, capital, or character to honor. Their word is their bond if they say it they mean it. If they can do something, they say it, and if they can't, honestly say that they can't. There is no room or time for those type of games in their life because they are busy enjoying all that life has to offer without the stress of consequences from not honoring commitments. Is that not sexy? How sexy is it that you know that you can depend on that person if you ever need them? If you call them, you know without a doubt, they will be there. If they can't, you never doubt them because they never lied, that's not in their character. This is good credit, and this is why good credit is sexy.

Is this not an attractive quality to have a mate? Someone who is dependable, honest, and reliable. Someone who honors all of their commitments and will never take on more than they can handle. Someone who is man or woman enough to say "No." Someone who understands and takes things in moderation.

This quality is attractive to banks and lenders also this is your applicant who receives the pre-approved credit card offers and loans as well as the non-solicited credit limit increases. The person who walks on the car lot and leaves with whatever they want with merely a signature. This example was an uncle of mine; he was so proud of that. I remember when I went to finance my first car. That bank wanted blood, and my uncle thought it was so comical. He said, "You'll get here one day." I didn't understand what he meant until I got older. I was risky, I never had any credit good or bad, so the bank had no idea who I was. Would I honor my commitment? Was I sexy or ugly, credit-wise? So they need proof of everything and a co-signer. My uncle talked about how the dealer would call him every two years or so and send him cars and just have him come in to sign for them.

This was because he was "sexy" to the banks. He had developed and proved his file over the years. He had every type of trade, mortgages, credit cards, car loans. He paid everything on time and never applied for anything he didn't feel the need. He lived in moderation at his means. He wouldn't co-sign for me, so I guess he didn't think I was "sexy" either.

Think of this story as if it was a blind date, you have no idea who this person is that you are about to meet. You haven't seen them nor do you have any mutual friends. They tell you they are the perfect man or woman and they want to be with you. How can you believe that? What do you use to validate this is true or false?

Hopefully, by now you can see where I'm going with this and why I've developed "Credit Score Dating." The principles that we've discussed up to this point are tools that you can use to help you in such a situation. Of course, that and meeting someone on creditscoredating.com. Yes, I had to plug my site, I think I did well this entire time. In any case, being serious again, understanding the correlation between credit, love, and interpersonal relationship can help to protect your heart.

What other ways are good credit sexy? What about my cousin's saying we talked about a little while back, the soldier in a tattered uniform? While granted, you may find soldiers sexy or people in uniform for that matter. How about the qualities of someone who have experienced things and recovered? Someone who may have experienced financial hardships or stress and made a recovery, which is now reflected positively in their credit score and report. Is this sexy, resilience?

Personally, I love to see a woman who doesn't let life or situations beat her down. Even when things get tough, she bounces back and comes back stronger. This is especially true when considering a life partner.

We mentioned in the previous chapter that live, love, and finances, are a rollercoaster ride. With all the ups and downs, it would be beneficial to have a partner who would be tested in this situation and can handle them. While writing this, the song comes to mind my mother used to sing, "When the Going Gets Tough, the Tough Gets Going," by Billy Ocean. The song appeared in the Michael Douglas movie, "The Jewel of the Nile." The movie was an action and adventure movie that remains one of my favorites to this day. It features Kathleen Turner as the damsel in distress if you will.

I mention this movie and song for a reason. If you think about serious relationships, they are like movies. Like movies, there are always climaxes, which makes the film interesting. There are good guys and bad guys, heroes, and heroines. Has there ever been a movie where the hero has come away unscathed? Has there ever been a movie where the hero has never seen any action? No, Of course not, that makes the film more realistic and believable. Also, there is an attractive quality in a hero or heroine that is experienced. How sexy is a person who can take the lead and does it well? I don't think it's attractive to someone not knowing and trying to lead. It's also sexy for someone not to fold under pressure but stand up and rise to the occasion. People are only able to do this with experience.

CHAPTER 10 - BRING THE SEXY BACK!

We talked about the "sexiness of credit" as well as some of the challenges of credit or credit that are not "sexy." Let me further iterate that having bad credit shouldn't stop you from dating. Whether you have bad credit or the person, you're dating; this does not have to be a deal breaker. The point that you should have noticed throughout the book, or the, as DJ Khaled would say, "Major Key," is communication.

Let's talk about if you or your mate has bad credit for any various reason. As I'm often asked, "How do I bring my credit's sexy back?" It all begins at the core, that is knowing where you stand and why. Once you make that determination, you can start addressing the issues. Much like my response to that previous questions, I pose the question, "How can I fix a house if I don't know what the damage is?"

Even if the credit was damaged by lack of care, the fact that you or they want to correct the credit is a great sign. This shows acceptance, accountability, and responsibility. These are mature qualities personally as well as in a relationship.

Take the time to revisit the problems that may have damaged the credit. I mentioned earlier, as it relates to the score, it is measured by several factors. Take a look at your file and see which factor is causing the most trouble to your score.

With the advancement of technology, a person can get their score and the factors that affect them on their phones. There are many sources to get this, from the credit agencies to your bank.

Just as in repairing your credit, similarly you can turn that relationship denial into an approval. Even if a person is ready to be denied for things unrelated to credit, like something about them that bothers you. Discuss what it is or how it originated. Is this something that can be repaired? This could be anything, little quirks that you don't like about them. Especially, significant things like commitment issues.

If you or they have money management issues that have led to bad credit. Talk about that issue, why does it exist? Is there anything that can be changed? Living about means, not saving, etc. How willing are you or they willing to work to correct the issue?

If the credit issue is because of debt, why? Is there a way to plan to eliminate the debt more aggressively? Is more debt being accrued at the same time? If the credit issue is payment related, why are payments not being made on time? Why weren't they paid on time in the past? Is there or was there a shortage of income issue? Can a stricter budget be put in place? Is there a budget established at all?

These are examples of places to begin in getting credit "sexy" again. Focus on the behavioral things and controls that may cause credit issues. We all know the definition of insanity, so it seems because most of us do insane things by definition. That is, doing the same thing frequently, expecting different results. Much like other problems that we may face, the solution lies in us most cases.

I mentioned before that there are cases where there are inaccuracies in the credit report that may have an impact on your score. Like the other issues, you won't know unless you review your file periodically. If there is an inaccuracy, the credit reporting agencies have processes established for you to dispute them.

CHAPTER 11 - FINALLY, FOR LOVE OR CREDIT

So, we've made it to the end. Hopefully, you've made it to the relationship you deserve. If your credit wasn't sexy, hopefully, it is now. So what now? I've been asked, "Are they with me for love or credit?" In fact, some people ask if the website attracts people to other singles solely for credit. I would love to say there aren't people who are looking for just that.

Unfortunately, this is not a perfect world, and there are dishonest people. Some people use people for everything from sex, money, and in this case, credit. This is for you to determine and protect your heart, credit, etc.

Your heart and your credit are precious, so you should always treat the two as such. Banks and lending institutions rely upon analysts, underwriters, credit bureaus, etc. to mitigate the risk of loss. You should do the same, and this is why I've written this guide. I want to arm you with a resource and tools as a "Love Underwriter" to underwrite the potential candidates vying for your heart and love.

Hopefully not your credit or anything superficial and material. You are a fantastic person, and if someone is chasing after your looks, money, or credit, they are missing out, and that's on them. Your value lies in what's under the surface.

A beautiful friend of mine said,

"I'm working on me, so I have more to bring to the table than just my looks. Beauty fades, and material things don't last. But the things that make me internally, like my love, my heart, and my mind, last forever."

When you're confident in you and your capability to love, you can love, on your terms confidently. Just as if you have good credit, you can pretty much buy what you want, when you want. You can freely make these purchases confidently without fear or denial or excessive verification.

Typically, people who have good credit are disciplined not to buy things are restrained not to buy things without reason or cause. Similarly, people who love themselves don't settle or jump in and out of relationships, just because. They know what they want out of relationships and wait to get it. This is because they understand their value, they know what they "bring to the table."

This may be from trial and error, whether it was work on them that needed to be completed or adjusting their expectations of others. Once again, you can't appreciate the best if you never experienced the worst. This goes for you, relationships, other people, work, credit, finance, etc.

Let's talk about love,

"Love looks not with the eyes, but with the mind. And therefore is winged Cupid painted blind."

William Shakespeare stated in "A Midsummer Night's Dream." With that saying no matter how powerful or potent it may feel, true love is smart.

"Love is that condition in which that happiness of another person is essential to your own."

Robert A. Heinlein stated in "Stranger in a Strange Land."

From this, I take that we need to be smart in love and prepare ourselves to make sure we are able to keep our significant other happy. Adding stress is not happiness, fighting over finances and receiving denials for this we want and need is not happiness.

This is the sexiness of credit, just as I explained to David Holland, "Security is sexy." Being secure that when problems arise even if we don't have the resources to solve, we have each other thinking on the same level. We are compatible in every capacity, including finance. We are secure and confident as a couple to make purchases, not just any purchase, but the right investments that won't affect our relationship. It's sexy to be with someone who loves you enough to love smart and work for our happiness.

I'm a proponent of "Love." In reality, I'm what some would call a "hopeless romantic." I've learned, however, just as Shakespeare stated, love, is smart. I wanted to find a solution to the problem that plagues most relationships, finance.

Everyone needs true love, it feeds you more than any nourishment; you feel full in the presence of love. But there's a vast difference between love and true love. True love knows no depth. It's an endless tunnel that sweeps you up in the whirlwind, and you're never quite free from it. It stays with you. And you hope this person will too. Falling in love is similar to falling in a big pool of warm chocolate. It's exciting, warm, and engulfing.

Falling in love is probably the best thing that can emotionally happen to a human being. It's a wonderful feeling. It's euphoric, the high that you never want to come down from. You're happy, at peace, and satisfied with your partner. No, that is an understatement, this is the one". "The one" you've dreamed of, the one you dream with, the one you dream of and act those dreams and fantasies out with.

There really isn't anything better - emotionally - than falling in love. In fact, it affects us physically and mentally as well. The irony is that it sometimes causes us to make "goofy" mistakes. I like to call it the "Hitch effect." Yes, Hitch, like the movie starring Will Smith. If you've seen it remember how he was perfect with his words, actions, and guidance, that is until he fell in love himself. That's when he made his mistakes which were comical to watch.

However, I find truth in it, we may be the best wordsmiths, planners, organizers, etc. So well put together, until we meet our match, our true love, and "fall." We become tripped up, tongue-tied, and even downright "stupid." It's really intriguing the way the heart, body, and mind works. I like to think it's our way of showing "the one" our flaws, so they know what and who they are receiving with no filter. So they can accept us for us if they are our "True Love" they should reveal theirs as well, and we find a certain peace within this bond of calamity.

It's really indescribable like the feeling of creating a child. You're passionate, caring, and more protective of your partner. You want them all to yourself. It feels like you could live with this feeling forever. You change and become a better person, for that person. In fact, you become a part of that person as they become a part of you. Aspiring to live as one, flaws and all happily ever after.

My daughter, Aunye, has developed the pattern of doing all of her work, projects, etc. from hardest and most time consuming to the least. She also attacks the project that would be the most difficult immediately. For instance, if the assignment is due at the end of the month while being assigned at the beginning, she will complete it the day assigned. This allows her time to make changes and perfect it without haste. She's a bit of a perfectionist, but she gets it honestly.

I looked at this and told her how smart it was. She responded,

"Daddy, it just makes sense, to get the tough stuff done first, so I'm not waiting until the last minute. I'm able to get all my work done correctly without rushing to have more time to do what I want to do."

There's something to this, not just because my daughter is an honor student. However, if we apply here the strategy to life and relationships, how much stress can we eliminate? How much time will we have to enjoy and learn ourselves and each other?

In relationships the same is true, this is why I've spent years perfecting the algorithm to attack the biggest problem in relationships. This is why I have written this book. Let's address the issue or potential issue in the beginning so our relationships can grow.

Geraldo Rivera stated in an interview we did together,

"You're a young man or woman you want to get married, you meet someone like you. You begin to hook up and get serious, and you find that he or she has $75,000 in college loans outstanding. So your life is starting off with a handicap, not only are you taking on the person, but you're also taking on a real financial burden."

In a news segment that we were on together, John Bussey of The Wall Street Journal stated:

"That's what this is really about right Niem? This about kind of getting one more indicator of the other person's values. It does not just see if their solvent. It's kind of generalized indicator of their values."

To answer the question titling the chapter,

"Is it for love or credit?"

The answer is both, use credit as a tool to love smart and protect your partner while ensuring your happiness together. That is the sexiness of credit.

RESOURCES

I've compiled some contacts to assist you in either keeping your credit sexy, making it sexy, and maintaining its sexiness.

Credit Reporting agencies:

Equifax Credit Information Services

Equifax Credit Information Services, Inc

P.O. Box 740241

Atlanta, GA 30374

www.equifax.com

Disputes:

Equifax Credit Information Services, LLC

P.O. Box 740256

Atlanta, GA 30348

Phone: 866-349-5191

Experian PLC

P.O. Box 2002

Allen, TX 75013

www.experian.com

Phone: 888-397-3742

Disputes:

P.O. Box 4500

Allen, TX 75013

Transunion

Transunion LLC

2 Baldwin Place

P.O. Box 1000

Chester, PA 19016

www.transunion.com

Phone: 800-888-4213

Disputes:

Online: https://dispute.transunion.com

Phone: 800-916-8800

Monday - Friday

Hours: 8 am - 11 pm EST

Closed on major U.S. Holidays

Free Annual Credit Report:

Your rights to your free annual credit report:

Federal law requires each of the three nationwide consumer credit reporting agencies - Equifax, Experian, and Transunion - to provide you with a free credit report every 12 months if you ask for it

https://www.annualcreditreport.com

Credit and Financial Counselors

Financial Counseling Association of America (FCAA)

611 Pennsylvania Avenue, SE

#1600

Washington, DC 20003-4303

www.fcaa.org

Phone: 866-694-7253

Credit Scores and Report Monitoring

Credit Karma

www.creditkarma.com

Credit Sesame

www.creditsesame.com

Quizzle

www.quizzle.com

Credit.com

www.credit.com

Fair Issac Corporation (FICO)

www.myfico.com

Capital One CreditWise

http://creditwise.capitalone.com

Discover Credit Scorecard

www.creditscorecard.com

Government Contacts

Federal Trade Commision

600 Pennsylvania Avenue, NW

Washington, DC 20580

Phone: 202-326-2222

www.ftc.gov

Consumer Financial Protection Bureau

PO Box 4503

Iowa City, IA 52244

Phone: 855-411-CFPB | 855-411-2372

www.consumerfinance.gov

ABOUT THE AUTHOR

Niem Green, also known as "The Daydreaming Mogul," is an entrepreneur, writer, motivational speaker, consultant, and manager. Born in Philadelphia, PA, he spent 10 years in the financial sector specializing in lending, risk analysis, and project management. Green would later go on to make a name for himself in the field of dating and as a published author.

Niem, or "the Mogul," cites the ability to "act his dreams out with open eyes," as one of the primary factors to his success.

In 2009 he released "The Daydreaming Mogul's Guide Vol. 1 Daydreams and Success. The book explored his philosophy on how to achieve one's desires through the power of daydreaming.

Niem is working on released the book called, "Credit Score Dating - the Sexiness of Credit." in 2016. Green previously developed this concept for his social media site creditscoredating.com where users pursue romantic partners with an emphasis on desired credit score standards. Niem and his credit score dating site have been featured on NBC's "The Today Show," in addition to Fox, the New York Times, Reuters, ABC and many more influential outlets globally.

Niem's passion for helping others and spreading his "open eyes" philosophy led to the creation of the "Young Daydreamers Foundation," One of the initiatives of the foundation is the program Niem created, "I Have a Story to Tell." The program aims to promote literacy by helping children in local schools and community centers create their own books. Besides improving their creative writing skills and reading comprehension, the program equips the kids with the necessary tools to achieve both short and long-term goals. The program has also blossomed into a music program and a photography program.

www.ingramcontent.com/pod-product-compliance
Lightning Source LLC
Chambersburg PA
CBHW031534260326
41914CB00032B/1797/J